WHY CAN'T WE ALL JUST GET ALONG?!

A RECIPE FOR SUCCESS IN YOUR RELATIONSHIPS

DANIELLE MACAULAY

What Women Are Saying...

"Danielle has courageously tackled a topic close to the heart of every woman - relationships! *Why Can't We All Just Get Along?!* brings practical, biblical and encouraging insights sure to improve and enrich every woman's life."

~ *Pam Farrel, International Speaker, Author of 46 books including best-selling Men Are Like Waffles, Women Are Like Spaghetti; and Red Hot Monogamy*
love-wise.com

"Experts say that women need other women. Yet, life experience says that women often hurt, judge, belittle and condemn other women. Obviously, something's wrong.

In her book, *Why Can't We All Just Get Along?!*, my good friend Danielle Macaulay identifies this disconnect and with refreshing transparency holds up a mirror to her own mistakes and ah-ha moments. As she reflects on this plaguing question, Danielle gently delves into the hearts of broken girls, revealing the image of what could be... whole women living in unity, cherished by a God who dearly loves His daughters."

~ *Ann Mainse, Heart to Heart Marriage & Family Ministries*
Author, Speaker, TV Host of A Better Us, Former Co-Host of 100 Huntley Street.
abetterus.tv

"Danielle is an extraordinary woman whose heart beats with the passion to help people live their lives with power, grace and joy. In her new book, *Why Can't We All Just Get Along?* she covers a topic that many have been afraid to touch - relationships among women.

If you have ever struggled in a friendship, this book is for you! If you have wondered why you have such a hard time with jealousy and competition with other women, this book is for you! If you have longed for deep, trustworthy friendships - then this book is for you! And while you are at it - buy a copy for all of the women in your life! What a gift it would be if we all just got along!"

~ *Carol McLeod, Best-Selling Author and Speaker, Author of StormProof, and Pass the Joy, Please!*
carolmcleodministries.com

"This book will bring laugher and truth to anyone who reads it. Danielle speaks from the heart and tells it like it is. The book will make you take a look at your own relationships and understand the dynamics of not just getting along but flourishing in relationships! At the core of this is the love of Christ and his commandment to love one another. I highly recommend everyone read this!"

~ *Robbie Raugh, RN/Nutritionist/Speaker/Author of The Raw Truth - 7 Truths to Health and Fitness, ESPN & WDCX Radio Host of "The Raw Truth".*
robbieraugh.com

"You'll laugh, cry and maybe throw the book down, but there's no way you can read this book and not react! Danielle's taken years to write and rewrite this book so it's a well-marinated steak with lots of flavor and meat to chew on! I was honored to be one of the contributors and share just a wee part of my story in getting along with girls in the church.

I know you'll be inspired as much as I've been by Danielle's latest book - the way she shares her hard-sought-after wisdom (how'd she get so smart, so young?) along with the many voices she's invited into her growth path. *Why Can't We All Just Get Along!?* is a recipe for sisterhood success!"

~ *Sherry Stahl, International Speaker, Soul H2O Blogger and Author of Water In The Desert, VP of operations of WIMM (Women in Music and Media)*
sherrystahl.com

"Danielle is full of wisdom! I appreciate her courage to challenge women to stop judging one another and to remember that Jesus bled the same blood for "her" as he did for you and me. This book will change your relationships with women around you and draw you closer to the heart of Jesus as you begin to view them like He does."

~ *Brooke Nicholls, Multiple Canadian Gospel Music Award winning vocalist and recording artist.*
brookenicholls.ca

"Danielle is unafraid to share her own personal struggles in relationships with women and the tension that shows up many times - often within ourselves. I appreciate her honest, and sometimes comedic, approach to this topic and her heart to challenge women to prioritize the bigger picture behind the power of strong relationships in the church over our own insecurities and preconceived notions."

~ *Emily Long, Fitness Coach, Speaker and Blogger*
theresolvedlife.com

"As a mom of a fourteen-year-old girl, the all too common issues with girl's have not changed one bit. When I first started leading women's events I would often say 'I used to never like women. I always had guy friends'. Until one day I learned the truth behind that statement: I just didn't want to do the hard work of getting along with other women, so I chose to hang out with the guys.

Women need each other. We are all on the same team. We can be each other's best cheerleaders if we learn the necessary tools in getting along with one another. Danielle's book will help you do just that and you will be a better friend for it."

~ *Angela Mercer, Music and creative assistant, Gateway Church, London, Ontario.*
angelamercer.com

"*Why Can't We All Get Along* is a candid view how broken relationships can be restored. Danielle's descriptive narrative of humor, honesty, and truth meets women where they are and takes them where they need to go in life. She uses scripture to enable us to find resolution for better relationships.

Thank you for taking the mask off, Danielle, so we too can take a revealing look at ourselves. This book is a 'must read' for moms, mentors, counselors, and life coaches. Don't miss the great recipes in the back of the book!"

~ *Pastor Linda Penn, CEO of Todays Living Hope, Inc. Todays Living Hope radio host on WDCX 99.5 FM & 970 AM* todayslivinghope.com

Thank You

Thank you, to all the women who lent their voice, their wisdom and their recipes to this project! Your partnership allowed many points of view to be heard.

Thank you to my "group text" prayer girls. I am grateful for your prayers and encouragement throughout this process. Lord knows I needed it! Thank you, most of all, for your friendships.

Thank you to my editor, Bill Farrel, and his amazing wife Pam. You two are quite an incredible duo! Pam - you're definitely the "ideas" girl, and you had some great ones for this project - you're amazing! Bill - I will be forever grateful for the time you took to, not only elevate this project far beyond where I could have taken it but, nurture my skills as a writer to help me find my "voice". Your guidance through this project was an extraordinary gift and your belief in me was tremendously encouraging. Thank you both for choosing to invest in me as a young writer, for championing me and believing in me. I am truly humbled and grateful.

Thank you mom for your help with proofreading - I owe you a pedicure and a big fat piece of cherry cheesecake. I love you.

Dan - When I told you I felt The Lord leading me to write a book (and I wasn't a writer), you said, "So, write a book!" And, from that point on, you never questioned my call or my ability. It's awesome how we take turns believing in one another more than we believe in ourselves. For that, for all your technical and creative wizardry, and a trillion other reasons, I love you.

Dedication

For: Terri and Tara,
for all your influence and prayers,
and for getting along with me so very well.

Contents

Section 4 - What Happens When We All Get Along

Section 5 - Recipes

Some of my Favorite Women
Share Their Favorite Recipes!

"Girls can be downright mean and women can devour each other and Christians can crucify each other, and I just keep telling my girl that: Girls can rival each other, but real women revive each other, girls can impale each other, but real women empower each other. Girls can compare each other, but real women champion each other."
~ Ann Voscamp, The Broken Way

Introduction

I am painfully aware of every idiosyncrasy, shortcoming and character flaw I possess. You will soon find out I am full of them. I suppose my redeeming quality is that I want to do something about them. I want to be better. I know my Heavenly Father wants this for me too. You may have heard the phrase that God loves us just the way we are but He loves us too much to let us stay the same. I am thankful that over the years He has gently poked and prodded me to mature - to become a woman who can heal and find freedom from many of the "spoilers" in this book and pursue the vast benefits of "getting along" the way Christ intended us to. But, I know there's more work to do.

If this book is in your hands, I am guessing you want God to work on you too. I pray the content in-between it's covers will motivate you to grow into a woman of confidence, love, grace, and character who reflects Christ in her relationships. It's a tough task. When we dance with people, we'll eventually step on their toes and get ours stepped on as well, but the dance is still beautiful. God doesn't want us to be wallflowers who stand on the sidelines of life. He's created women to intermingle for his glory and invite others into the dance.

Unfortunately, we often isolate ourselves and others with

our thoughts, actions, attitudes and words. And, dang, we can be downright mean to one another. It's not just you, and it's not just me. We've all been there. Our self-esteem, relationships, and quality of life has been spoiled by judgement, pride, jealousy, envy, comparison, competition, insecurity, misunderstandings and unforgiveness.

"The Housewives of Orange County" paved the way for a parade of popular tv programs that glorify women who are nasty, catty, deceptive and manipulative with one another. Millions of women sit back with popcorn and entertain themselves with "friends" who are unfriendly with one another. Rather than fight this natural tendency, we are glamorizing a lifestyle of backbiting, belittling and battling with the women around us and we are encouraging a rising generation of girls to create division, confusion and lots of heartbreak.

Sadly, the women of the church often aren't any different. The first time I heard the words "I hate her" directed towards me was in a church bathroom just as we were about to go out and praise the Lord. If a camera followed us all around, they may very well compile enough content to create the next big hit: "The Housewives of First Baptist, New Covenant and First Assembly".

My years of being involved in church life have proven to me that Christian women struggle to get along just as much as women who don't yet know the Lord. Perhaps we're just better at keeping it under the radar by wrapping our mess up in a prettier, more spiritual bow (I know I was).

I finally decided enough was enough. I asked the Lord "WHY can't we all just get along?" After praying that prayer, I started to see things differently. I began to believe that we really *can* get along with all our differing opinions, personalities and temperaments. The relationship truths I discovered in God's word unraveled me and convinced me God has a better way- Go figure! So, this book is going to untie that bow and let the mess spill out so we can work on cleaning it up and prevent further muck and muddle. My hope is that we follow Jesus' example of how to treat one another so we can be a gift to one another; not a grievance.

Ladies, let's keep the drama on the big screen as we build one another up in real life to be better together. Let's finally figure out how to . . . get along.

As you work your way through, you will see a couple icons that signal to you some important aspects of this book. Here they are, so you can make yourself familiar with them:

I Wish I Had Known...

"I wish I had known" is an entry from another woman I know personally, and whose opinion I highly value (and some are from me). Imagine that you and her are sitting down for a cup of coffee and she is able to share her insights with you. She will reveal to you what she wishes she had known when she was younger about the topic pertaining to the chapter she is a part of.

Reflective Questions

"Reflective Questions" are just that - questions I ask you that you can reflect on in response to each chapter. My intent is that you are able to apply this book to your own life and get max benefits from it, which means not just reading about my journey, but looking inward as well.

Here we go!

We've All Been There

Its not just me and you who have struggled. Listen to other women candidly share their struggles too:

> *"I was an outsider, left out of social events, bullied at school and treated this way even in the church I called home"*
> ~ Young girl, eager to belong, and be involved in her youth group.

> *"I look at women, and think why can't God make me like her and then I get depressed and don't want to leave my house."*
> ~ Teenage Christian girl, defeated and isolated.

"I look at myself in the mirror and instead of being proud of my slightly stretched out body, I hate it. I feel like I'm not good enough."

~ New mom of twins, who thinks she's only one who battles these feelings.

"My sister-in-law and me have this unspoken jealousy/competition thing going on. It makes me mad! What should I do to help myself not compare our lives, kids, money and our families?"

~ Fed up woman, wanting resolution and restoration.

"My jealousy of other girls is so bad that I started starving myself and self-harming just to escape the pain and reality that I'm not one of them"

~ Young girl who has not been set free by God's truth

Perhaps your situation and experiences are different, but I am certain that at some point you have felt what these women felt, and that your relationships have suffered because of it. If you identify, then turn the page and get ready to toss these spoilers in the trash. First we'll explore how these spoilers bring ruin to our relationships, but then I'll provide a Biblical recipe that will ensure the sweetest relationships that will satisfy and bring Glory to our baker...I mean, our maker. Don't be surprised if I pepper in some humor along the way...

Relationship Spoilers

I love to bake and I have some pretty stellar recipes. When I get it right, the kitchen smells awesome, I am pleased and others get to enjoy the delicacies. If, however, I get just one thing wrong, it can ruin everything. One bad egg or rotten milk can spoil an entire batch of cookies. I once made a pot of chili, and somehow left out the chili powder. It was not too appetizing! And, dont even ask, what food tastes like when you mix up cinnamon and cumin.

Our relationships are the same way. When you get it right, they add incredible memories to your life and make everyone feel more valuable. The introduction of just one spoiler to the mix, however, can bring ruin to you and your relationships. Let's make sure to leave them "out of the bowl" from now on. You and her weren't meant to be like oil and water - you were created to be emulsified, woven together and unified for God's glory.

In my research of the spoilers, I discovered that some of them surprisingly contain elements that can add health to our lives, but (not surprisingly) Satan has turned them and used them to rot our relationships. God takes what Satan meant for evil and turns it into good, but our enemy does the opposite. He takes good things and spoils them so that they spoil us. At least 4 "spoilers" discussed in this book *do* have a healthy side, if we can nip the bad parts in the bud and turn them around for good.

Take **prejudgment** for example - often those who are prone to judge the most are ones who may have the gift of discernment. My husband often relies on my "gut instincts" about people, but if I'm not careful I can easily head south into the land of judgement.

Pride has a good side as well. Healthy pride motivates and encourages others. It says "I am so proud that you accomplished your goal" or "I am proud of myself for earning that promotion. I worked really hard." Unhealthy pride though, proclaims we are better than others, and boasts "There's no way she could ever do that as well as me."

And then there's **envy**. Could there be any good in it? Envy can be steered in the right direction too - towards inspiration. It says "Wow! She is amazing! I want to be just like her!" It makes you want to be better - just not better *than her*. Unhealthy envy causes wallowing, and doesn't actually make you better at all. In fact, it makes you feel a whole lot worse.

Comparison can be handy when we keep ourselves in check. It can help us look to others and learn from them, then push us to strive to be better. It highlights what needs to be changed or improved. Ultimately, Jesus is our measuring stick and the one to whom we must compare ourselves. Comparison becomes unhealthy when we develop a sense of pride or sink into a state of insecurity, depending on the results.

Competition can be healthy when it causes you to become your best self. I love playing volleyball with athletes who are better than me because I find I rise to the occasion and perform vastly better when I compete alongside and against them. If we didn't have competition to propel us to the next level in our grades and our workplaces, the productivity and level of excellence would plummet.

You can see that many of these spoilers don't necessarily have to ruin us! When we relate to women in a godly way, and view ourselves with godly confidence, we don't have to let the spoilers spoil us.

The rest of the "spoilers"; **jealousy, insecurity, misunderstandings** and **unforgiveness,** are simply downright relationship toxins; akin to the chemical preservatives that are tossed into boxed "food". We are led to believe they are there to preserve us, but over time and in the end, they do us in.

As you continue on in this book, resolve to toss the toxic parts of these spoilers and embrace the elements that can be useful to you and beneficial to others.

Section 1
RELATIONSHIP SPOILERS

CHAPTER 1
Prejudgement

"Don't judge a book by it's cover. You may miss out on a good story". ~ Unknown

Do not judge, and you will not be judged. Do not condemn, and you will not be condemned.
~ Luke 6:37

Long Jumping to Conclusions

I was surprised to find out that we judge others in the first *six* seconds of our interaction with them! (Catrina Welch, *Confident Beauty*)[1] Do you believe this? Now that I think about it, I sure do and it gives new force to the old saying, "Don't judge a book by it's cover." I'll be the first to admit that I'm guilty of sizing another woman up before she's even had a chance to speak to me. It's ok. You can admit it too. We are prone to prejudging more than we realize. We look from afar and decide a firm opinion on why she is the way she is. There are countless times I have assumed the worst about someone, judged them before I really knew them and have written someone off coming out of the starting gate. Here are examples of the absurdity we surmise in our brains during those 6 seconds:

She's overweight = She must be lazy.

She's on a stage = She must be full of herself.

She's with HER = She must be a snob.

She's a blond bombshell = She must have great self confidence.

She's toting that high-end purse = She must be materialistic.

She's always smiling on Instagram = She's living a charmed life.

Sometimes our immediate gut instincts are bang on, but more often they can be *way* off base. There was a time I was so off base I was out on the warning track. I made all the obvious assumptions about a woman too early on as I judged her based on her outward appearance. I made assumptions because of her lovely and lively dinner parties in her white picket fenced home. I presumed perfection and surmised she must not have a care in the world...or at least nothing like mine. I was wrong. When I got to know her intimately, I discovered her burdens were deep too. Her pain and struggles revealed she was more like me than I had given her credit for. I know I'm not the only one who belongs in the dugout when it comes to summations about other women. We've all struck out when it comes to our assumptions...

I Was Totally Wrong About You

I recall with a chuckle a night towards my final week of college. It was exam week and things were wrapping up at the small Bible College I attended.

Students had dwindled from the dorm rooms. Our particular floor of girls had whittled down to just a handful. The friends I made were no longer there and loneliness set in. I noticed a couple other girls who were also now without their regular group of friends. They noticed me as well so they invited me to hang out. Until that night, I had known their names and faces and their reputation as a fun and comical duo, but that was it.

We sat and chit chatted, laughed and, ok - gossiped a *little*. We had a great time. Comical is only the half of it. They were downright pee in your pants hysterical. They were down to earth and friendly and I think they figured out I was as well. That night became a favorite of my entire college experience.

As we were winding down, giggles still surfacing from our bellies, one of the girls blurted out:

"Before I knew you, I thought you were a snob....but, I was *totally* wrong about you."

"Oh...that's ok." I quickly responded, trying not to seem taken aback.

I quickly moved on, hoping to not draw out the awkward moment. I decided to simply take her admittance as a compliment. I had, after all, proved them wrong. I shrugged these comments off in the moment but they left me thinking afterwards...

What a shame that it took us all year to find one another and figure each other out. We had a blast of a night, but it took way too long to get there. Perhaps it's because some initial "sizing up" got in the way. It wasn't until the empty halls shoved us together that we realized we could have been friends all along - if we had given each other a chance.

This night taught me to give others the benefit of the doubt. If I could lay aside my initial "6 second size up," I just might see who people really are sooner..

What *Assuming* Makes Us

Perhaps we can expect sorority sisters to make inaccurate assumptions about each other, but what about women with a few more years experience? While arranging details for a conference where I had booked my husband Dan to lead worship, the director completely caught me off guard.

She asked me, "Is there anything stirring in your heart to share with these women? Would you be interested in being one of the keynote speakers for the event?"

I was confused because I was just the booking agent. What did I have to say to these women? This was just around the time, though, that the Lord had burdened my heart about writing this book. I knew I had to do it.

I actually heard myself say, "I would be honored to be one of the keynote speakers. Thank you for asking."

Then, as my senses came to me, waves of nausea set in. I asked myself, *"What have you done, Danielle!? What have you done?!"* I knew that this was a "God" thing but I was completely out of my comfort zone. After all, I had been a keynote speaker at exactly *zero* women's conferences. I nearly picked up the phone several times to say this was a mistake, but thankfully I didn't pull the trigger.

In preparation for the event, I was asked to send a bio and recent picture. Hysterically, I sent in an incredibly unprofessional headshot (can anyone say "selfie"?) and a paragraph of all my "achievements" (like, enjoying HGTV while changing poopy diapers). This would go immediately under my husband's high resolution photos and bio with a laundry list of accolades, experiences and famous people he's "shared the stage" with. I wondered if the women would take me seriously or just assume I was there via nepotism. So, there you have it - it was set in ink that I was a joke.

The day of the conference began with much fear and trembling. Remarkably, I spoke confidently about much of the content of this book, giving special attention to our tendency to judge one another. It helped that my hubby was cheering me on while he functioned as my techie powerpoint guy. It was obvious as I ministered that the words hit home. It was a powerful service and I heard from many women that it was just what they needed to hear. That day was confirmation for me that the mess God had cleaned up in my life would be used for His glory and that He would equip me with all I needed to use it for good.

The most powerful moment for me came completely out of left field. As I was wiping my brow in relief that my portion was over (and it wasn't a train wreck), the other scheduled speaker took the stage for the next session. She was a distinguished Southern preacher's wife in her mid-fifties. As she approached the microphone, I remembered her put together and scholarly looking press shot. This definitely wasn't her first rodeo. I couldn't wait to hear what she had to teach. But, instead of diving into what she had prepared for the women, she took a big breath, stood humbly in front of us all, and admitted that my message was indeed for her too.

Whoa.

I sat stunned as she confessed publicly how she had sized *me* up upon receiving the promo package for the event. She had assumed things about me from my "selfie." She admitted in front of all the women that she was guilty of sarcastic thoughts such as,*"Look at this cute little tart. I'm sure she'll have wisdom to share."* She even confessed having sarcastically thought *"Oh great - I get my old lady pic right beside her gorgeous photo in this pamphlet. Hoorah. Sis boom ba."* And then, boom- I spoke about the dangers of pre-judging and comparing ourselves to one another.

How incredibly strong of her to admit weakness in front of a room full of women ready to receive God's word from her. It was astounding to see how God used two broken vessels that weekend. Our transparency set the stage for breakthroughs in women's lives - glory to God!

Innocent Until Proven Guilty

I wonder if I have missed out on friendships of gold because I decided too early on I had someone figured out.

I loathe the all too common conclusion, *they were not for me,* especially in moments of loneliness. Who could have been there for me that I shoved aside too soon?

Rather than playing the judge, I should let the jury hang a while and hope for the best. I must choose to make that stranger my sister by looking at her the way Jesus does - with grace, hope and a whole lot of love. We all bleed the same underneath that judge's robe. And, Jesus bled for us all.

So, take a second (or six) to ponder who you may have judged in a fleeting moment. Understand that judging won't just spoil a relationship, it will prevent one from blooming.

My friend Sarah illustrates that it is possible to pre-judge yourself, not just others, and create a barrier to living out God's plan for you.

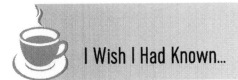

I Wish I Had Known...

...Not to pre-judge *myself!*

"I was the kid who couldn't get my hands on enough 'business stuff'. I loved playing 'store' and was particularly excited when my parents' latest interest in Amway, Shaklee or any other 'side job' waned. Why was I so eager? The extra supply of order sheets, carbon paper and notebooks were quickly disposed of and became meaningful components to make my store legitimate. It was fun to pretend!

I graduated college with a business degree and landed my first job in sales/marketing. I was married at 29 and had no idea I would be 37 when our first child was born.

After having a baby, everyone started to ask... "What are you going to do? Are you still going to work?"

It almost seemed ungrateful or dismissive for me to consider working. I imagined people saying in private, "After God answered her prayer for a child, how could she go back to the sterile, calculating, cut-throat business world?"

But that wasn't God's plan for me.

I went back to work after four months at home. My husband decided to leave his job to be home full time with our son. So here is the struggle. In our society, the modern working woman has only been accepted over the last generation. And only in the last 10-20 years have we seen more fathers stay home as the mother moved into the workforce. I find the Christian community seems to lag with the thinking or expectation that a working mother can't be synonymous with God's best plan.

So while I sometimes struggle with being a good mom, wife and Christian, I have learned that my own view of stereotypes and a few peoples' reactions caused me to question what God had designed and purposed me to do in life. He made me and created me with specific intentions that were clearly there as a child.

Looking back, it's always clearer, but I wish I would have

recognized His design earlier so I could take hold and not question His plan."

~ Sarah King

God's plans are always best and He has called us to be connected to one another. The first six seconds should never be the defining moment of any relationship!

 Reflective Questions

~ Can you think of a time you judged someone too quickly?

~ Who in your life is not at all what you initially "sized them up" to be?

~ When have you let another's judgements and opinions about you define your decisions?

CHAPTER 2
Pride

"Pride will always be the longest distance
between two people."
~ Unknown

Look beneath the surface so you can judge correctly.
~ John 7:24 NLT

Pride has a Dark Side

Pride is a beast that can motivate you to action or maul your relationships.

Pride can be a great tool for helping others see their value. After all, we pat our kids on the head after the baseball game and say that we're "proud" of them. A smile forms on our faces when our boss tells us the same. We get a warm fuzzy when our teacher passes our exam back to us with a wink. She's proud of that A+...and so are we. Having a sense of pride can be a positive thing. Pride encourages us to maintain standards of excellence and reinforces positive self-esteem. As we tell others we are proud of them, it builds up their confidence and self-worth as well.

So, why is pride something we need to be wary of?

Let's begin with the wise words of Solomon in Proverbs 16:18, "Pride goes before destruction, a haughty spirit before a fall." He also warns us that God opposes and has no use for the proud (3:34) and there's more hope for fools than proud people (26:12). When it comes to our relationships, it is best to let others praise us and not our own lips (27:2) as we remain humble; thinking of others as better than ourselves (Phil 2:3).

These warnings exist because pride has a very dark side. Dictionaries use the words "conceit", "arrogance" and "haughtiness" to capture its negative potential. The clincher for me was, "Inordinate opinion of one's own dignity, importance, merit or superiority". This is exactly the opposite of humility, which The Bible says we are to possess (Phil. 2:3). Seems to me, plain and simple, that pride should be a term we reserve to encourage the accomplishments of others. When we evaluate ourselves with pride, we run counter to the kind of woman Christ is leading us to be. So, yes - pride has an ugly side.

Noble or Defective Pride?

If pride can be both good and bad, what differentiates a noble sense of pride from a defective one? It is our recognition of the *origin* of our blessing and our declaration that every good and perfect gift comes from our Heavenly Father (James 1:17). We must pause and evaluate:

Do we remember who gave us our blessings, or are we caught up in the majesty of ourselves?

Do we think that we are better than others because of those blessings, or do we recognize that it is God who equipped us with the ability to think, perform, and acquire?

Do we accept that apart from Him we can do nothing?

I think of the image of a lioness proudly strutting her stuff for all of the jungle to see. You can picture it, right? We've all seen those women walk by us in the mall, the office - even the church lobby. They've got something we don't and they're happy about it. Their turned up noses prove it. They make sure even their nostrils are higher up than ours. It is such a turn off, isn't it?

Queen or servant?

"Do I think I'm Queen of the Jungle?" I ask myself.

I'll keep it real. Sometimes, yes.

I certainly have pitiful, pride-filled moments. On occasion I have walked through the doors believing I am the smarter, more godly, or most attractive one in the room. I occasionally come to the twisted conclusion that others should be gazing up in awe at me because I am somehow better than them. My snooty snout has been upturned on many occasions.

What about you? Have you strutted your stuff through

your jungle? Have you hoisted your nostrils up into the air? Do you make attempts to come across more important than you really are? Do you have moments of conceit, holding yourself in the highest esteem; that of a Queen?

Remember - pride comes before a fall.

This is precisely why Jesus emphasizes humility and servanthood. He knows it's the better option that lifts everyone up. In her startling book *Interrupted*, Jen Hatmaker bares her soul. In chapters like "Becoming a low life" and "Get off your high horse - Jesus", her transparency spoke to me:

"Consequently my love for others is tainted because they unwittingly become articles for consumption. How is this person making me feel better? How is she making me stronger? How is he contributing to my agenda? What can this group do for me? I am an addict, addicted to the ascent and thus positioning myself above people who can propel my upward momentum and below those who are also longing for a higher rank and might pull me up with them. It feels desperate and frantic, and I'm so done being enslaved to the elusive top rung…getting to the top requires someone else to be on the bottom…it's a ridiculous game where everyone is either scratching your back or stabbing you in the back, depending on whether your rung is either above or below theirs." [2]

Counter to what our arrogant egos crave, Jesus knew that abundant life awaits us at the bottom, and it's shockingly peaceful down there. (Plus, no one can see up your nostrils, which I think is a bonus.)

That pride, which keeps us reaching for the top rung,

breeds competition with others and, more frighteningly, with the Lord. You may have found that most women do not want to share their spotlight. But, more crucially, God says he won't share his glory with anyone. It's foolish of us to think we can get a piece of that pie. We may try but we will never succeed without consequence.

Don't let Jesus fall off your back.

My husband and I will never forget the first conversation he had with my sister's new boyfriend, Miguel (now husband). Dan was trying to describe his job as a worship leader to Miguel, who certainly didn't speak the "Christian-ese" language we've become so accustomed to. It was all foreign to him. He pondered for a while and then profoundly responded:

"So, you're kind of like the donkey that carried Jesus to all the people for his triumphant entry?"

Whoa. I guess he knew more of his bible than I had given him credit for.

Stunned, Dan replied "Ummm yeah, I guess I kind of am".

Miguel continued with the next part of his profound thought process, "I think that when donkeys get proud and puffed up, they kick up their front two legs and stand up on their hind ones in order to get higher....so, make sure you don't let Jesus fall of your back, ok!?"

We fell silent for a moment, processing a thought we knew we would never forget.

Now, we may not all be a Sunday morning worship leader, but in a way, we are all that "donkey". Our job is to humbly present Jesus to the ones who surround us. We may not be four feet higher in the air on an actual stage, but our Christ-following lives are certainly on display for all to see. Our actions and attitudes can lead to Jesus' triumphant entry into other's lives. When we become prideful, however, and puff ourselves up, we will knock Jesus right off of His rightful spot.

Some days, perhaps at a larger event or somewhere I know he has a few fans ready to sing along with him, I'll give Dan a friendly little reminder not to let Jesus fall off his back, and that he's just a ... "donkey", after all. Really, aren't we all?

I'll say it again - pride is a beast; a pompous lioness; an arrogant ass. Ultimately, she's a liar. She makes you believe it at the time, but it is never worth it to "strut your stuff" for other women to see, if it means you let Jesus "fall off your back."

> *"Be humble, thinking of others as better than yourselves." ~ Philippians 2:3*

My friend Shelly candidly shares about how a prideful comment directed towards her, and then her own prideful response, built walls around her heart...

I Wish I Had Known...

...That pride will divide

"I remember the moment like it was yesterday. I was a new parent and had arranged a mom's morning out for the young moms in the church. I was soon to be heading back to work after my maternity leave and I'll never forget the comment that was made in my direction, "I'm staying at home with my kids. I didn't have children for someone else to raise." I felt myself sink into the floor and later as I quickly gathered up my son to head home, the guilt was overwhelming. That experience put up a wall in my heart. I decided that I wouldn't let anyone get too close, and my pride prevented me from being open and connecting with other moms in the future. Thoughts would always run through my mind – *I don't need friends. People don't understand my life. I'm working and showing my kids that I can do anything.*

Looking back, I wish that I hadn't let a comment hurt me so much, and I wish that I didn't allow pride to define my future relationships. The truth is, we are all on different journeys and no one's journey could ever be the same as someone else's. Over the years I've learned that loving and respecting the choices of others is the best way that we can support one another and prevent pride from overtaking our relationships."

~ Shelly Calcagno

Reflective Questions

~ How do you think others perceive you when you've acted like "Queen of the Jungle"?

~ What are some of the moments you've "let Jesus fall off your back?"

~ In what ways does pride spoil your relationships?

CHAPTER 3
Jealousy and Envy

"Envy grieves. Jealousy Rages." ~ Mason Cooley

"What is causing the quarrels and fights among you? Don't they come from the evil desires at war within you? You want what you don't have, so you scheme and kill to get it. You are jealous of what others have, but you can't get it, so you fight and wage war to take it away from them." ~ James 4:1, 2

Evil and Disorder

Where there is jealousy and selfish ambition (aka envy), you will find evil and disorder of every kind (James 3:16). Can I get a witness? I am willing to bet my typing fingers you have seen this - even within the church walls. In my church experience, nearly every issue that arises between people boils down to one thing: jealousy. Our enemy knows that if he can stir up these feelings, evil and disorder of every kind will follow, including:

- Malicious and vicious talk
- Gossip, lies, deceit and manipulation
- Immature and foolish behavior

- ◆ Pouting, and focusing on the negative, blaming God
- ◆ Rage, malice and vindictiveness

Danielle Too

Jealousy got the best of me when I was a soon to be, blushing bride.

Now, don't get me wrong, Dan and I were in love and eager to be married. There was a moment, though, when I am sure he thought he was engaged to the Wicked Witch. We were in a large Canadian department store choosing the items to be placed on our gift registry. We gallivanted around the store, price scanners in hand, firing away. We had fun choosing and dreaming. The fun, however, came to a hostile halt in the kitchenware section where we found some charming serving trays.

"I think we should put this on the registry for serving coffee and dessert," Dan suggested.

The glare I served up, turned the environment ice cold. "When do *I* ever serve coffee and dessert on a serving tray?", I fired back.

You see, we knew a woman who did. She cooked and entertained like Martha Stewart with the warmth of Laura Bush and likability factor of Julia Roberts. She regularly collected fifteen friends by her cozy fireplace and fed them four star meals. I felt measly in comparison. I dreamed of being that debonaire. I was threatened by her superior talent. After all, I could barely figure out a Betty Crocker brownie mix.

My fear that Dan wanted a woman like that - not someone like me - made me insanely jealous. As much as Dan tried to convince me the tray didn't matter, my jealousy clouded all clear judgement. My voice was dripping with disdain as I announced, "I will never serve you tea and crumpets on a serving tray. *Never.*" Dan sighed and laid the tray gently back on the shelf. Needless to say, it never made the final cut on the registry.

I know I'm not the only one who has lost their mind to envy and jealousy.

Kings and Priests

King Saul was ravaged by his jealousy over David. Initially impressed, he was comforted by David's talent that resulted from the favor bestowed on him. When others began to celebrate it, however, Saul's heart erupted. After killing Goliath, the women of Israel shouted, "Saul has killed his thousands and David his *ten* thousands." Rather than rejoicing with them, "Saul was very angry." (1 Samuel 18:8) His approval swiftly turned to abhorrence at the thought that David was more popular. Saul sought to remove the threat that his position of powerful, beloved king could be torn away.

I don't blame Saul for his initial pangs of jealousy. After all, who would want to publicly come up short and then hear others sing about it? Rather than brush off the peanut gallery, Saul internalized the comparisons and kept a close and "jealous eye" on David (1 Samuel 18:9). He soon became a tormented, raving lunatic. The women planted the seed, but

Saul watered it until jealous roots dug deep into his heart. He embodied these verses to a tee:

> *"Anger is cruel and wrath is like a flood, but jealousy is even more dangerous."~ Proverbs 27:4*

> *"A peaceful heart leads to a healthy body, but jealousy is like a cancer in the bones"*
> *~ Proverbs 14:30*

Even religious leaders became jealousy's prey. Philippians 1:15 tells us that some were "preaching out of jealousy and rivalry". In Acts 5, high priests had the apostles thrown in jail because they were jealous of the miraculous signs and wonders they were performing. You'd think spiritual men would be elated that people were being healed and set free. When their position was threatened, however, jealousy dug its heels in as fear trampled their good intentions. As far as they were concerned, *they* had the right to bless and heal people and they would share the privilege with no one. Clearly, none of us are exempt from the threat of a jealous heart.

Waging War Within, and With Others

In her book, Jealousy and Envy, June Hunt explains the difference between jealousy and envy: *"Envy is empty hands craving to be filled. Jealousy is full hands fearing to be emptied."*[3] Envy craves what others have. It is a burning desire to *get*, fueled by a sense of entitlement. Jealousy, on the other hand, clings to what it has. It is a burning desire to *keep*; fueled by a sense of retaining control. I like the way urban dictionary describes the difference:

"If you want your neighbor's new convertible, you feel envy, and if she wants to take your husband for a ride in it, that makes you jealous."

Both are toxic and will demote us to desperate, whiny, cranky versions of ourselves, like a child who's been forced to share her doll. Jealousy makes us unhappy, angry, suspicious, delusional, bitter and resentful. A familiar human experience, it has been observed in infants as young as 5 months of age. Everyone has faced it at some point but few fully respect its power to turn Kings into Court Jesters, Priests into Pharisees and believers into the belligerent. Even the most influential, anointed, spiritual and otherwise jovial of us can be crippled under its weight and tempted to trample our sisters in Christ simply because God has been good to them.

If you feel like you've got these saboteurs in check, consider the words of Dr. Meg Meeker:

> *"Jealousy can be as benign and gentle as an irritation. I have found myself annoyed by a (woman) (even if she's really nice) when I am jealous...there are twinges of irritation, anger, and annoyance, as well as a desire to gossip, backstab, or criticize, when we first feel jealousy...We who are jealous hurt more than anyone because it is a dull state of self-torment."[4] ~ The 10 Habits of Happy Mothers*

Deceived by What we Perceive?

Dan proudly recounted to me the time he played

"Balderdash" with friends at his Bible College. The game has you guess the definition of a bizarre or uncommon word. One player shares the correct definition but others make up fake descriptions to throw opponents off. He says that every female in the group "bit" on his bogus definition of the unknown word. His answer was *a women's intuition*. Unaware of his pandering, every single one of the women fell for his nonsense - hook, line and sinker. He giggled with glee to me as he said "I guess their women's intuition was off that night."

I would like to suggest that our "women's intuition" can be off sometimes, ladies. Much of what we envy in others is actually not possessed by them at all, so we often deceive ourselves. Even more, the enemy lives to deceive us and will pander to our preconceived notions.

We live in an edited and polished era. Phenomenons like Facebook and Instagram allow us to create a retouched world for others to see. Even without these technological wonders, the percentage that others truly see of us without our "masks" on is quite low. Pastor Steven Furtick says that we tend to compare "our behind the scenes with everyone else's highlight reel". It's so true. If you come to my house and knock on my door at 8am Tuesday morning, you won't encounter my profile pic - the one with the cheerful look-ing girl, whose hair is blowing in the wind. Nor will my house resemble the spic and span version displayed in the background of my son's birthday photos on Instagram. My intuition tells me you too, are not spontaneously remarkable.

Envy's Half Truths

A gorgeous and talented young girl admitted to me that she was envious of my "perfect" life. What!? I nearly choked on my cheerios that morning. She had some confusion about my illusion, but I quickly revealed my reality to her. I assured her that she really didn't know all the ins and outs of my life. Come to think of it, that very day all hell was breaking loose at the Macaulay house. Greasy and un-showered, I had just finished lashing out at my husband as my kid was having a teething fit, all while I was attempting to unearth the counter from a pile of dishes. My life was far from idyllic.

This young girl only witnessed me all prettied up in a Sunday morning church bow. The extent of her interactions with me was two full hours of the 168 hour week. Other than that, she had the "highlight reel" of my Facebook account to consult. After quickly debunking her theory, I shared the scene that was unfolding as I read her message. I told her that I too, had envied other women's highlight reels but was beginning to understand there's more to every woman's story. I reminded her that what she sees is "the best case scenario" of my life which is why she'll never see these types of posts on my Facebook wall:

Insufficient Funds in the grocery store line. #oops

Totally bored and lonely. How come you all look like you're having fun?

Stomach's a churnin' - Shouldn't have eaten that Mexican. #trots

Stayed up anxious half the night. Today I can barely function.

Just popped zit. I know... I shouldn't do that. #couldntresist

That all happens, I'm just not shouting it from the social media rooftops.

But, what if the woman we envy really *does* possess the things we long for? The truth is, there will always be someone prettier, skinnier, wealthier, trendier, more popular, talented or educated. But, envy doesn't tell you the whole truth. Here's a thought that envy doesn't want you to consider:

Envy will idealize and glorify what someone else has, but downplay the struggle it may have taken to achieve and maintain that which you are envying.

Sure, she has the dream house but her husband is rarely there, because he's out earning it. She got the part you wanted in the school show, but you didn't see her defeated after previous rejections. You're envious of her size 4 waist, but you don't see what it takes for her to maintain a petite frame.

Green with Envy

Perhaps the one you envy truly is living an enviable life. She is happy and content. Her blessing will turn your stomach if you are green with envy. We are in dangerous territory when we can't rejoice about another woman's accomplishments, or we find pleasure in her misfortune. This was precisely the Wicked Witch's intent for Dorothy. She did everything she could to snatch those ruby slippers from under her feet. The witch was not only mean, she was miserable. Bertrand Russell got it bang on when he said,

"Of all the characteristics of ordinary human nature, envy is the most unfortunate; not only does the envious person wish to inflict misfortune and do so whenever she can with impunity, but she is also herself rendered unhappy by envy. Instead of deriving pleasure from what she has, she derives pain from what others have."[5]

"Envy rots the bones." ~ Proverbs 14:30

I Wish I Had Known...

...To turn envy into inspiration

"There is a better way. When we "love others as ourselves" (Matthew 22:39) and "rejoice with those who rejoice" (Romans 12:15), we touch the heart of God and make strong connections with others. When envy pangs begin to creep up, I now ask myself, "What about her success *inspires* me?" I wish I would have done this all along.

It immediately shifts my thinking from "I am a victim and they are the enemy" to "I am learning and they can teach me something here! What do I need to learn?" Instead of resenting that person's success, I have discovered a willingness to honestly *cheer* for them! And I will tell you what... it feels amazingly better than secretly resenting their success and happiness. Cheering others on requires honesty and humility but being empowered by their blessing beats the emptiness of envy any day!

So I challenge you to ask yourself... The next time you see someone who has achieved the body results you want, or is having the work success you want, or marriage and family success... *"What about her success inspires me? What can I learn from her?"* It will change everything!

~ Emily Long

Reflective Questions

~ Who in this chapter most reminds you of yourself?

~ What are the drawbacks/hurdles/obstacles the women you envy might face?

CHAPTER 4
Comparison

"Comparison will be the number one thing that will keep you from doing what God's calling you to do."
- Kari Jobe

The Comparison Trap

I was feeling pretty darn good, as I stared at myself in the mirror.

And then, I went to work out class…

"Comparison is the thief of joy", Theodore Roosevelt said. Ain't that the sad truth?

A fulfilling life is one where we connect with people - not compare ourselves to, or compete with them. But, all of us fall prey to comparison, perhaps even unconsciously. Nonetheless, we put other women under a microscope and dissect their lives piece by piece; and then see how each piece measures up against us. Sometimes we feel superior about our findings. Usually we dread them. Neither make us happy, because when we stack ourselves up against one another, we are exactly that - against ourselves, and against one another.

Back to the mirror - I was feeling pretty good about myself. I didn't mind what was staring back at me ... until work out class, that is. There is no easier way for a woman to fall into the comparison trap than to stand in a room with thirty other athletic chicks, surrounded wall to wall, floor to ceiling, with *mirrors*. It is an invitation to dejection. All of a sudden, the image in the mirror that was attractive in isolation now seemed distorted and disfigured..I didn't like it at all!

At the front of the class stood an amazingly sweet instructor who unintentionally made me feel bad about myself. She had quite a few years on me, more than twice the amount of kids as me, and a way waaaay tinier hiney than me. For one whole painstaking hour, we were all doing the compare stare. You know what I'm talking about -- stare at the instructor, stare at yourself, stare at each other, then repeat often enough to feel bad about yourself. All the while, we were sweating through our spandex, attempting burpees and mountain climbers, pretending we weren't in excruciating pain. What else was going through my mind (other than the pain) was a stark realization of how pale I am compared to the rest of the bunch. Now I know why that girl referred to me once as "Snow White". It was code for "honey, you sure are pasty!" Oh, and yup, I couldn't help but notice that my hips are larger than that 20 something chick at the front left, who's killing it with every move. There's no way not to notice that I'm not jumping as high or lunging as low as the entire front row. NO WAY. And, that, my friends, is deflating. Ugh. Caught in the comparison trap once again.

And, I fell in. Hard.
My joy was officially stolen.
I know that I'm not alone here.

The Uphill Battle

In my "scientific" research for this book (social media), I asked women on Facebook what they compare about themselves to other women. You name it and we compare it -- our careers, how we raise our children and our house cleaning/cooking capabilities; our clothes, our weight, our sex appeal and how our husband treats us - even our spirituality. We compare everything from our families to our fingernails.

But, we can't fully put the blame on ourselves. We live in a competitive world. Everywhere we turn, we are encouraged to scrutinize each other. American Idol paved the way for this generation to master the art of picking people apart and comparing the intricacies of their looks, talent and personality with the "competition". Popular celebrity gossip magazine "Us Weekly" regularly includes a *Who Wore it Best*" page, featuring two women side by side, wearing the same outfit. Viewers are encouraged to vote "who wore it best." The writers analyze features from beads to bags, butts to boobs and everything in-between. Is there really ever a winner in these games?

Comparing ourselves with others is not only a losing battle, it is downright sin. It pronounces us the judge (it's not Simon Cowell's job, and it's not ours either). It produces a critical spirit and prevents us from growing into the women

God created us to be. Comparison infects the garden of your heart with weeds that choke your self-worth. It tills the ground for both *pride and insecurity* to grow.

The Comparison Criminals

These products of comparison are true bandits. *Pride* sneaks in the back door of your heart, when you over focus on yourself, and what you have more than others. It snatches up your humble heart. *Insecurity* barges right in the front door when you over focus on what you don't have compared to others. It strips you of your confidence. Either way, you've been robbed, and in the blink of an eye, you've burgled yourself from a contented life. Even a queen was reduced to bitterness and misery when she asked *"Mirror mirror on the wall, who's the fairest of them all?"*.

God doesn't want us so over focused on others that we take our eyes off Him. *He* is the lens through whom we must judge ourselves against, and girls He is *never* against us. He is *always* for us.

Comparison will not only royally suck the living joy and goodness out of you, it will keep you from all the incredible things God has in store *just* for you.

Comparison Prevents Promises

You may have heard of some folks called the Israelites. They were famous for being cranky and hungry while stuck in a desert for waaaay too long, even though God told them they would make it out and inherit an abundant place. Canaan, the land God promised to them, had everything they dreamed of - a far cry from their current living conditions. They needed to get there, and fast! In order to take that land for themselves, conquering current inhabitants was required. A couple handfuls of men were sent to stake out the land to see what they were up against. What the scouters found was not good news. The place was teeming with what seemed like giants to them - healthy and strong men who lived in fortified towns. In comparison, they saw themselves as a people reduced to eating a few fish and nibbles of bread while wandering in circles. Caleb and Joshua were confident they could succeed in their mission so they encouraged Moses to have the Israelites "take the land." Unfortunately, the others had already come to their own conclusions:

"They are stronger than we are...
***Next to them**, we felt like grasshoppers...*
Let's just turn around and go back into the desert."

They did it too - just like me! They stacked themselves up against other people and came up short. They were deflated and defeated before they even began. As soon as they decided they didn't measure up, they called it quits and were ready to walk away from all that God had planned for them. Their comparison conquered them before any giant could, and it was about to keep them from The Promised Land.

How about you?

- Have *you* let comparison keep you from *your* "Promised Land"?
- Have you thrown in the towel, because next to *her* you just didn't measure up?
- What have you missed out on because you concluded you came up short?
- Who are you wasting too much brain power on?

It is true - you may feel like a "grasshopper" next to others. Maybe she is prettier, smarter, more successful. Maybe she really does have it all together, and perhaps she is living the dream - and you are not.

Is it because you are spending too much time exploring, or "scouting out" the ladies who you believe are living in their "bountiful land"?

The Israelites spent 40 days checking the Canaanites out. And yes, they were strong, but that strength did not make the promise of the Lord null and void in the lives of the Israelites. They had already overcome Pharoah, the most powerful ruler in the world at the time. In the desert, God led them - a pillar of cloud by day and fire by night. He sent manna. He promised and He provided. He was now leading them into something better than they'd ever experienced before.

The Israelites were His chosen ones who saw miracle after miracle, and yet, when they faced people who made them feel like tiny insects, they completely threw in the towel.

Comparison's Cure

There were two men who didn't give up, though. One of them was Joshua. He was confident in the Lord's capabilities, despite current circumstances, so he chose to believe in God's promises. And, I think I know why.

Rewind back many many years to when Joshua spent time in the presence of the Lord. Exodus 33 tells us that each night Joshua stayed in the tent where the presence of God was…and he stayed quite a while. In that lingering, is where Joshua learned who God was, and who He created Joshua to be. Joshua fixed his attention on God, and there his identity was formed. It was *there* that his confidence and his faith grew bigger than the Canaanites. In the face of the giants, Joshua knew who he was, and he was no grasshopper.

Lovely lady, you are God's chosen one. Stop for a minute, breathe and let that sink in. He thinks *you* are the fairest of them all. Don't let the mirror tell you anything else.

Another woman's looks, abilities, book smarts, family upbringing, position… none of that will ever negate and nullify the person God created you to be and the specific goals He's planned for you. Do not look to the left or right. Stop peering over at others. Resist scoping out the competition. Don't let the giants intimidate you or keep you from receiving what God has to give. Cling to the one who is bigger than the giants and live in your own Promised Land.

*"For I know the plans I have for **you**, declares the Lord, plans to prosper **you** and not to harm **you**, plans to give **you** a hope and a future!"*
~ Jeremiah 29:11 (emphasis mine)

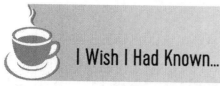

I Wish I Had Known...

...To close my computer and open my Bible

"The link showed up on my Facebook page one morning and I was surprised by how instant and guttural my response was. It was the link to a soon to be released book authored by an incredibly eloquent, fantastically sweet (I had met her in person!), instantly likeable woman whom I had heard speak at a conference several months back. She was not just a good speaker, but a 'knock the ball out of the park' kind of speaker to boot! As I read her profile and glanced at her perfectly chaotic family photo, my heart lurched a little bit. She was a beautiful Christian woman and had somehow seemingly figured out how to do "it all" while I sat at home struggling to get the dishes done and figure out how to add a Twitter widget to my small, poorly designed, unread blog. I was envious. Very envious.

When I think about this little thing called comparison in light of a bigger thing called relationship, I realize how detrimental it can be—especially within the church! God does not want that for us, and more specifically God does not want this for me. He calls me to something greater -- contentment in my season of life and gratefulness for the blessings I do have. I am called to trust that he knows the desires, dreams and wishes of my heart and has a plan for my life that will most likely look very different than that of her life, and her life, and her life.

When I find myself in moments like that, I'm increasingly aware how much I need a perspective shift - a God-sized perspective shift. *I need to close my computer and open my Bible* and soak in the promises that God has for me. I am learning to take my eyes off myself, and off other people, and place them back where they belong...on Him. I wish I realized this years ago!"

~ Lisa Littlewood

 Reflective Questions

~ What have you been distracted from because you have been too busy "scoping out" other women?

~ Describe your "Promised Land".

~ What is unique about *you*? (Describe the special/ unique qualities, attributes and specific calling God has blessed you with.

CHAPTER 5
Competition

"A flower does not think of competing with the flower next to it. It just blooms." ~ Zen Shin

Myth Buster

I used to think that men are more competitive than women. I have since concluded that myth needs to die. It is not just men who have ambition to triumph over their competition - women do too! The difference is in *how* we compete. Since men are bubbling with testosterone, they tend to be more aggressive and are driven by a strong need to succeed. Estrogen influences us to be more relational and drives us to be accepted and connected. Men are not more competitive than women, we simply compete over different things.

We want to look the best, perform the best, have the most well-behaved children and get picked to sing the solo. We dress to impress the other *women* at the party more than our husbands or other men. We filter our faces and our families to appear the most well put together on social media. Simply put, we want to be on top and we want to win- badly! But, if we continue competing against one another, our relationships will spoil. No one wants to be around a woman who makes them feel like a loser. I hope this part of the book will challenge each of us to consider areas where we can let others win. Before you think about that, I want you to imagine a beautiful garden...

Weeds and Thorns

I have never met a gardener who enjoys their weeds. Those pesky, relentless, unwelcome intruders choke out pretty flowers and productive plants. Weeds usually spread like wildfire, offering no grace to the beautiful blooms beside them. In fact, they often suck the life right out of them. Weeds, one could argue, compete for space and the spotlight in a garden.

I also am not aware of anyone who appreciates thorns. They are hard, rigid and painful, but hard to avoid if you're preparing a lovely bouquet of roses. We would all rather do without thorns and weeds. And yet, when we compete with other women, we are weeds and thorns to them. We choke out, or become a "thorn in the side" of our competition. We scratch and claw, leaving wounds. We incessantly aim to overrun her beauty, fighting for more turf in the garden. But, ladies - there is *room enough* for us all.

Room To Bloom

There is room for us all to bloom.

God's garden is big and He has created us all uniquely

beautiful.

Philippians 2:3-4 instructs us to value others above ourselves; to do nothing out of rivalry, and to look to the interests of others. This, essentially, is giving others room to bloom.

My all time favorite flowers are Peonies and Lily of the Valley. Both are captivating to me but very different. Peonies are gigantic, stunning shouts of color. Only a few are required to create a breathtaking statement of a bouquet. Lily of the Valley display tiny, dainty blossoms while they emit a strong fragrant scent. These small flowers are known to spread well, like filler. They may not be noticed as quickly as a larger, brighter bud, but in my garden I make room for Lily of the Valley. They don't need to prove themselves to me or fight for attention. I already know they are breathtaking. On top of that, they are special because they remind me of my Grandmother, whose backyard was filled with them for too short of a time every May.

While you may feel smaller, maybe like "filler" compared to a majestic Peony of a person, your Maker wants you to know that He planted you purposefully, and you are beautiful. Your aroma and the details of your features please him. You are special. Don't feel the need to overpower another flower. There is no competition.

In fact, the most exquisite bouquet to me is a mix of Peonies *and* Lily of the Valley. They compliment each other, elevating one another's beauty. This is how God; your gardener, wants you to see yourself in relation to the ones around you - stunning on your own and able to stand up tall beside another flower; creating something majestic.

From a Chart to Your Heart

"But, isn't competition sometimes 'healthy'?" someone suggested to me. I understood what she was saying. Our world uses competition as a vehicle for improvement. When we compete for a job, a coveted spot on a team or top mark on an exam, our desire to beat out an opponent definitely adds fuel to our fire. I have found in my life though, it is healthier to compete with *myself* more than with others.

When aiming high, remember that a "personal best" mentality is healthier than a "stomp on the rest" mentality. Ask yourself, "Am I doing better than *yesterday*?" instead of "Am I doing better than *her*?"

We women like to turn everyday activities into a competition that certainly don't need to be! We view the girls around us as slots on a top 40 radio chart. We, of course, are aiming for that coveted #1 spot but, if we can't get there, we at least want to be one slot above our direct competition.

What if we stopped looking at the women around us as rivals and, instead, viewed them as our *relatives*? The women you seek to overrun are your sisters in Christ, ladies. And, they experience the same hopes, fears and wounds as you. So, what if we sympathize rather than scrutinize? What if we personalize them instead of perform against them?

This is what will happen:

"If we view potential contenders as equally broken people with real problems, pains, hopes, dreams and disappointments, we will have taken the first step to unraveling a rivalry."[6] ~ Beth Moore

Yes, and amen, Beth! When we can personalize other women and understand they are more like us than not, we are able to love them so much more easily. This is why God says, "carry each other's burdens" (Gal. 6:2)...so we can drop the competition and begin to help one another. God knows we need each other so desperately. We are on the same team!

Same Team! Same Team!

One of our previous Pastors told a story about his son and daughter's soccer team. He described the typical scene of young, rookie players unsuccessfully chasing the ball in a swarm around the field. Not yet understanding the way the game is played and the benefits of a team, each child fought for the ball - even if it meant they were stealing the ball from their teammates. Their tactics were fruitless, other than stirring up frustration in everyone.

Fired up parents began yelling *"Same team! Same Team!"* to remind their young ones that it was not the name of the game to take the ball from a person wearing the same colored jersey. Girlfriends, I want to say the same thing to you - in bold and italics - ***"Same team! Same team!"*** You don't need to steal the ball from her. It's ok to let her win because, when she wins, you don't lose. We're all in this together. Unity accomplishes much.

"Do nothing out of selfish ambition or vain conceit. Rather, in humility value others above yourselves, not looking to your own interests but each of you to the interests of the others". ~ Philippians 2:3-4

 ## I Wish I Had Known...

...God's purpose for my friendships is more important than my own agenda

"As I look back over the people who have come and gone out of my life and out of the church, I can't help but wonder, *could I have made a difference in where they are now if I had treated them better?*

It had been a long and painful road to finally feel good about myself and have these close friends. Anything that threatened these relationships was quickly taken out. A couple of years earlier, the older students in the youth group should have known better to be kind to me and include me. I was now the older student and I think I knew less than they did!

A new girl came to youth group who was pretty and funny. Everyone seemed to like her, including the boy who at the time held my affections. This was my recipe for disaster,

I know! Instead of reaching out to her and making her feel welcome, my entourage and I quickly drew lines in the sand and covertly tried to get people to pick sides. She clearly became my competition.

While we never said anything to her face, I'm ashamed to say the verbal abuse she received behind her back was awful. Some of it, of course, got back to her through the grapevines. Needless to say, she was only in our youth group for a year or two before she left. She didn't go to another church and she isn't following the Lord now.

While everyone makes their own decision about following Jesus, what a difference I'm sure it would have made in her life to have walked into a welcoming group, to have been encouraged in her walk with the Lord and seen the love and acceptance of Jesus modelled in His followers. In the end, the only thing that matters is people knowing the love of Jesus and spending eternity with Him. It's not about who has the most friends or the most stuff. If we welcome people in, then we all have friends and no one is on the outside. I wasn't gaining anything by keeping her away. I still would have had everything I had before plus one more friend. I wish I would have known that the only score worth keeping is how many people I've helped snatch out of "the fire" (Jude 1:23)."

~ Dannie Phillips

Reflective Questions

~ In what areas are you most tempted to compete with other women? (Beauty, men, talent, motherhood, intelligence, spirituality, or another area.)

~ How has competing with women helped you?

~ How has it hindered you?

CHAPTER 6
Insecurity

"Until You cross the bridge of your insecurities, you can't begin to explore your possibilities"
~ Tim Fargo

The Devil's Demolition Derby

Insecurity is the vehicle that delivers us to the place where we judge, compare, become jealous and compete in unhealthy ways. Our enemy is undoubtedly behind the wheel. Satan uses our insecurities to drive us into the ground and drive wedges between us. He's not concerned for our safety. He's delighted when we feel like we're flailing and falling and fearful of what could happen next. He wants us alone in that car. He'll ram us into others and beat us up until we're bent and broken, our minds and hearts bruised as if we've been thrust into a brick wall without a seatbelt or airbag. He lives to keep us cowering and feeling unsafe. He *loves* when we're insecure.

Blind Spots and Lemons

My son loves - no, he's *obsessed* with - the Disney Movie *Cars 3*. The Demolition Derby is his favorite scene. "Miss Frit ter", a no mercy school bus, delights in showing the smaller cars "who's boss". She enjoys intimidating and laughing in the face of her opponents. The cars that participate in the derby end up smashed, bashed, crashed and trashed. Most of them are covered in mud until they're unrecognizable.

Ladies, have your insecurities ever made you feel bent and broken inside? Have they muddied your clarity of thought? Mine sure have. My insecurities have whispered and whined loud in my ears, "You're not as good, talented, liked or worthy as other women. Come on Danielle, admit it. Others are better than you." They've led me to believe I shouldn't trust. They've advised me to man-handle situations and people in order to feel in control. They've encouraged me to throw in the towel.

I want to let you in on a huge secret. Your insecurities are based on lies and intimidation. Satan, the Father of Lies and the intimidator that he is, has messed with you like that bully school bus. He's flung mud into your eyes so that you can't see who you really are. He's browbeaten you until you give up and feel like you don't measure up. He's convinced you that there's something or someone bad around the corner ready to take you down. It's not true.

Our insecurities are simply *blind spots*. A blind spot is an area where a person's view is obstructed. In the eye, the blind spot is the point of entry of the optic nerve of the retina, *which is insensitive to light*. In a car, our blind spot is the place we cannot see in our front, side or rear view mirrors. Satan works to keep our vision obstructed so we remain in darkness and insensitive to the light.

Insecurity is often due to trauma, mistreatment, rejection, humiliation or unsettling circumstances. Life can hand us lots of lemons, and our enemy uses those sour things against us. Have you ever gotten lemon juice in a cut? It stings! This is what Satan loves to do - squeeze acid on our open wounds to extend and maximize the pain. And then, he makes us fearful of feeling that pain again.

And so, *insecurity tells us not to trust God or others.*

Really, Satan is the one we should not trust. He wants us feeling riddled with flaws and defects, like a lemon of a car. But, friend, listen to me - there is no defect that God cannot fix. You are not so flawed that you need to feel unsafe or invaluable. God is our spiritual mechanic, and *He* is where we receive value and safety.

Defensive and Distracted Driving

Things have changed a *lot* in the twenty plus years since I took my driver's test. There were no iPhones or GPS screens. I didn't have two mini, yet extremely loud, distractions in the backseat fighting over the DVD controller. Life today is much more distracting for me than it has ever been.

I do, somehow, remember the tips my instructor told me about about "Defensive Driving". He said to be *aware* of my surroundings and *diminish my distractions*. Oh, if he only knew what the twenty first century would hold.

I believe, if we are to live defensively against our enemy, we must remember to do the same. We must get rid of that which will *distract* us. What in our lives diverts our attention from God and the security He offers us? What hinders us from staying *alert* to the enemy's plot to keep us cowering? Is it television or social media? Is it an imagination we allow to run wild? Is it someone in our lives to whom we have given permission to speak lies to us?

Who's in the Driver's Seat?

We know that Satan wants to control our minds. If he's got those, he'll steer us any direction he pleases. Of course, it will be the direction *away* from God's truth.

So, may I ask you a question? Who is in the driver's seat of your mind?

Are you searching for security in a man, a friendship, a facelift or financial bracket? You will never find it there. The only way for us to be truly secure is to listen to what God says about us. He is our security blanket and solid ground. He fills our gaps and heals our wounds. We can find safety and confidence in Him if we are willing to hand Him the keys and let *Him* drive the car.

Destination: Confidence

Many years back, I read a life-changing book penned by the incredible Beth Moore. *So Long Insecurity; You've Been a Bad Friend to Us* alerted me to the enemy's scheme to keep me insecure. I realized that Satan loves when we're insecure because it repels others from us and keeps us cowering in a corner. This incredible book made me aware of events from my past that were keeping me cowering and insecure.

I worked actively to *cross the bridge of my insecurities so I could explore my possibilities* by putting God in the driver's seat. I don't always nail it, but I am much more confident in my own skin and in my relationships with other women. My need to compare myself has softened. The jealous feelings of wanting what other women have are only occasional visitors. I am more content with the thought that I have something unique to offer and I can trust God to be strong for me in my weak areas. It is easier to see God as a Good Father who has given me good gifts and to see myself through new eyes - *His* eyes. I firmly believe that every woman can do the same. I strongly encourage you to hunt down that book and devour it!

Before Beth's book entered my life, I tended to view other women's successes as my failures. The biggest "light bulb" moment for me was when Beth said:

> *"When we work from an activated mentality of God-given security, we are fully capable of thinking another woman is beautiful without concluding we are ugly. We can esteem another woman's achievements without feeling like an idiot, we can admire another woman's terrific shape without feeling like a slob. Where on earth did we come up with the idea that we have to subtract value from ourselves in order to give credit to someone else?"*

It was as if Beth was hollering this right to me, shaking

my head to create a mental shift. I needed to be shaken up so I could begin to admire the beauty in others without questioning my own. I want this for you too, friend.

The best way I know to change my perspective is by renewing my mind through God's word. Romans 12:2 says *"Do not conform yourselves to the standards (or, patterns) of this world, but let God transform you inwardly by a complete change of your mind."*

Completing this book's corresponding Bible study "Get Along Guide" is imperative to changing your mind and understanding the truth about yourself. Also, feel free to re-route your journey through this book, and bypass other chapters directly to the "Quart of Confidence" chapter. It is filled with Biblical truth that will completely transform your thinking about yourself. I encourage you to do so!

I pray that as you fill your mind with the right thoughts and let Jesus "take the wheel", His GPS will navigate you in the direction of being a confident woman! When you are confident in who God made you, your possibilities are endless!

> " Let us then approach God's throne of grace with
> confidence, so that we may receive mercy and find
> grace to help us in our time of need"
> ~ Hebrews 4:16

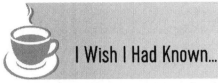

I Wish I Had Known...

...That other's opinions of me should not control me

"I've always been a people-pleaser. It's not something I'm proud of, but long-term, healthy relationships require that I deal with issues, not just gloss over them. As I gain a greater understanding of what God says about me, and a stronger acceptance of those truths, the opinions of others has less power over me. Earlier in life, I was almost completely controlled by people's opinions of me. If only I could turn back time!

I've learned that I cannot make relationships with other girls my first priority. No matter how good the girl is, she's human. Humans make mistakes, and hurt humans hurt other humans. If we rely on the opinions of others to determine our worth, we will live unhappy, people-pleasing lives. Understanding who we are in Christ sets us free! Now that I know what God says about me in His Word, I am a more confident woman - not proud, but confident in who God made me to be. I'm free to let go of unhealthy relationships and embrace healthy ones. I'm free to make decisions based on what's right, not what I think others want. I am able to leave places and not second guess everything I said or did. I'm free to pursue my God-given dreams and trust Him that I'll have what it takes to accomplish them. It's wonderful living free!"

~ Sherry Stahl

Reflective Questions

~ In what areas am I most insecure?

~ What is the biggest lie I have believed about myself?

CHAPTER 7
Misunderstandings

"Don't think too much or you'll create a problem that wasn't even there." ~ J Dix

The Brain Game

The mind is a wild place.

I'll admit it - I overthink *way* too much. I'm suspicious and awfully pessimistic. It's disgustingly true that my default is to think the worst of others as I ponder probing thoughts such as, "What is their agenda? What do they hope to gain? She must be selfish, because I know I am!"

While chatting with a sweet and spunky lady about the issues that keep us from "getting along", she suddenly summed up this relationship spoiler when she blurted out, *"Sometimes it's all just in my own stupid head"*.

Isn't that so often the case?! Sometimes that's *all* it is, girlfriends. Our conflict may just be all in our own imaginative, overly dramatic, overanalyzing, pretty little *heads*. Yes, there are occasionally legit issues between us that need to be worked out, but more often than not, our brains play games on us and we end up making mountains out of molehills.

I can remember moments when a flood of thoughts interrupted everything wondering why a friend hasn't texted me back, or trying to read between the lines of the text (a huge producer of misunderstandings), or why she becomes incommunicado for a while. A day of peace can easily be disrupted by swirling questions, *"Why didn't she bother to chat more, but just gave me a quick hello in the lobby of the church."What did I do? Did I say something?* I rack my brain to find an explanation.

Perhaps the reason is....most likely, it wasn't *me*. And, when it comes to the way other women act towards us, I will suggest, maybe it isn't *you* either!

I am Not the Sun...and Neither are You.

For some of us, more strenuous and challenging than calculous, are the painstaking moments when it registers (or worse, we have someone else help it register) that the world doesn't revolve around us. It would be beneficial for students to be offered a "How to handle life not orbiting around you 101" class. It would get much more use in daily life than quotients and derivatives. There was a time that my Good Shepherd revealed to me I was being a bit too irrational and self-absorbed...

We had just moved to a new town and I needed friendship. My first encounter with Janet was encouraging. She was slightly older than me but I immediately connected with and felt excited to get to know her. I needed someone like her in my life at the time and she fit the bill. I got a good feeling from her. She seemed to be excited to get to know me as well and expressed that she'd love to meet for coffee. We exchanged info the same day we met, and I looked forward to getting to know her more. We had really hit it off!

I reached out to Janet that following week to take her up on the coffee date. I waited to hear back... but I didn't. So, I tried again in another week. Nothing. At risk of coming off too clingy, I made one last attempt and left it alone after that. A bit later, I received a very short and vague email response saying it wouldn't work out right now, but hopefully another time. That was a blow off if I'd ever heard one! I became deflated, insecure, let down and a little perplexed. *What could I possibly have done to change her mind about me? Did I come on too strong? Had she somehow discovered something about me that she didn't like? Maybe she was humoring me from the start.*

My mind raced on and on, but still I didn't get it. I just had to accept that she was no longer interested in getting to know me, and move on. So, I did.

There's Always More to the story...and the Person Behind it

Devastatingly, I found out many months later that Janet was now caring for her husband around the clock because he was going through chemotherapy. Turns out, he had been diagnosed with cancer right around the time I met her. I did the math and it seems her world was being turned upside down the very week I was wondering if it was all about *me* (insert huge facepalm). This taught me a lesson, and I want to pass it on to you.

The moment your mind is reeling about a supposed situation with someone, diffuse your thoughts with this reality: the mind is a wild place and makes up wild tales. To make things even more chaotic, the enemy loves to help you write fictional guile and make you believe it as truth. So, give those mental battles to God and give people the benefit of the doubt. Realize that the problem might not be anything but that cute little noggin of yours. There may be another side to the story than you're perceiving. Or, sometimes there's no story at all...

Inadvertent Scowls

I was minding my own business, sitting in my car at a red light. A woman pulled up in the lane beside me. I glanced over to find her scowling at me and flipping me the bird!!! What the!? Classy, right? Shocked, I quickly set my gaze back towards the traffic light, pretending what I just saw was not actually directed towards me. As the advanced green rescued me from the moment, I sped off and caught a glance of myself in the rear view mirror. I had been frowning from the blinding rays of sunshine in my eyes. Sure enough, I was adorning a horrific scowl on my face! I had no clue I looked like that, because I certainly was not angry. In fact, I was in a decent mood. I had no reason to scowl at anyone. Her response to me was less than lovely, but I understand how she could have felt insulted. This woman must have assumed my demeanor was directed towards her, and she may have been asking herself what on earth she did to deserve that. The answer is *nothing*! Sometimes, what you think is an issue may not be an issue at all. It may seriously be *nothing*!

Positive Intent

I have realized along the way that pessimism is for the birds. It does no one any good to think the worst in others. Instead, I am learning to live a life with *positive intent*. My default doesn't always have to assume the worst - that her "scowl" is meant for me, that she is out to get me or using me for her own interests. Rather, when I think the best of someone, our relationship has the ability to thrive. And, when we choose to see the best in others, the best in us will be revealed.

We simply must think less about ourselves and what others must think of us, while we train ourselves to focus more on what others are going through. Ladies, if we spent less brain power wondering what other women think of us, we could actually keep up with our kid's Common Core math! Just imagine what else we could accomplish! So, what other people presume about us is none of our business. Our goal should be more about how we can affect others positively - not how they affect us negatively! I highly recommend three "maybes" and two "makes" that help keep my mind in check:

1. Maybe there's more to the story
2. Maybe there's no story at all
3. Maybe, just maybe, the story is even better than you thought!
4. Make the story about her - not about you!
5. Make the story about God's truth because Satan tells us lies.

Think well, my friend!

"Don't jump to conclusions - there may be a perfectly good explanation for what you just saw."
~ Proverbs 25:8

 ## I Wish I Had Known...

...To listen to my Father, instead of a liar or my own stupid self

"Dear Jesus, Women hate me. Amen." I literally have prayed that prayer. It's pretty stupid, but what can I say? I get stuck in stupid now and then.

Am I the only one who has ever felt that way? You know – when you walk into a room full of women or even a little circle of them – no matter what you say or do, it feels like they all hate you.

It's a childlike feeling, don't you think? Do I expect that Jesus will come down from Heaven, stand beside me in His splendor and glory, and alert the room full of skirts and heels, "Women, this is my child. Please, love her."

Can you even imagine? I really think that is what I hope for. But again, welcome to my stupid.

Jesus has never once made any blazing, protective

announcement for me but he has done something far better. He has taught me to listen to him. "My sheep listen to my voice." John 10:27a (TNIV)

When my child runs to me and says, "Joey hates me." My response is, "How do you know that is true?"

I have often heard God's words to me in the very words I have spoken to my children.

The lie we choose to believe about how we are perceived is as ancient as Eden. "Who told you that you were naked?" (Genesis 3:11) Yes, Adam and Eve were naked, but their shame was born out of sin. Our own broken perception is caused by sin, and only through the lens of Scripture can we view anything in this life correctly. A woman's broken perception of herself and other women is a powerful tool of the enemy geared toward destroying the body of Christ. I waste tears and words when I pray a prayer like, "Dear Jesus, women hate me."

We have a choice - common to ancient and modern women of God, and even encountered by our Savior. We can listen to the liar, or we can listen to the Word of our God."

~ Laura Lewis

Reflective Questions

~ Describe a time when your imagination led you astray regarding an issue with another woman.

~ Why does the enemy use confusion and misunder standing as a weapon against our relationships?

Now, what if there are big issues to deal with? What if a relationship really does suffer a genuine offense? I am glad you asked - we will discuss that in the next chapter.

CHAPTER 8
Unforgiveness

*"Harboring unforgiveness is like drinking poison
and hoping your enemy will die."*
~ Joyce Meyer

Toil, Trouble and Drinking Poison

"Double, double toil and trouble;
Fire burn, and caldron bubble."

In the famous story of Macbeth, three witches are in a
dark cave, casting a terrible curse upon a sailor whose wife
offended one of them. They were seeking their revenge...

Unforgiveness - it is universal, it is an evil poison, it is a
toxic cancer of the heart. It makes us scowl and seethe and
seek revenge. It gives us nightmares and steals our sleep. It
grits our teeth and grinds our souls.

If you want toil and trouble, then don't forgive.

When Your Best Friend Doesn't Show Up to Your Baby Shower

Life was good for the Macaulays. Our ministry job was

great, our little family was growing and our community of friends was loving and supportive. Then, in an instant, *it all blew up in our face.* This story pains me to write because it forces me to relive the horror of being wronged and the pain that goes along with it. I now understand the desperate need to forgive.

I'll never forget the Tuesday afternoon Dan came home from the office with a solemn and sickly look on his face. He sat my weary, 8-month-pregnant self down in my son's powder blue rocking chair and told me he was out of a job. Yes, you heard right. He was let go from his pastoral position, just weeks before I was about to give birth. It literally came out of nowhere - and for no sensible reason. That agonizing moment was the beginning of an incredible series of losses. We were not just dealing with a job, but a community of friends, mentors, our home, our reputation with many who were unaware of the whole story, and a little loss in our faith and the goodness of Christian people. It turned into a terrible mess filled with lots of unanswered questions and feelings of betrayal. The way it was handled seemed so wrong but we were powerless to defend ourselves. We tried to make sense of it all but, honestly, we were lost. It was all so personal and and so incredibly unwarranted. The word implosion is the best way to describe it.

The only glimpse of light in the dark, blown up storm we were living was a new baby to be delivered. I tried my hardest not to let the pieces of the implosion hit my precious sons, one unborn and the other literally trembling in fear from the upheaval. I tried not to let it affect my already fragile, emotional, pregnant self. It was a near impossibility. I still remember not being able to sleep most nights after that due to a dull ache in my back and a piercing one in my heart. One night I went downstairs to make my time useful and began throwing glass dishes into cardboard boxes at 3 am because there was no way we could stay where we were. We had to get out. Exhausted, and feeling more alone than I'd ever known, I slinked down in a swelled up, beat up heap on the floor, praying for God to remove us from this hell. I needed someone - anyone - to come pick me up. My husband couldn't, because he was right down there with me. I needed a friend. I needed the friend who had picked me up on several other occasions. I needed Claire. But, she was nowhere to be found.

You see, in the midst of utter life shattering turmoil and the kind of betrayal and loss you don't understand until you've lived it, (which was a whole other lesson on forgiveness) I discovered that the one I had looked up to for years - well, I discovered Claire was *human*. My trusted friend, mentor, big sister type confidant was suddenly not there to confide in. While she was coming from a well meaning place, she chose to keep a blind eye to what had been done to me. And, it felt like she was choosing sides. Claire's grace filled justifications for my offender felt more like fiery daggers in my heart. She didn't want to know, and perhaps she feared the gory details. She seemed to have no interest in my part of the story (the hell I was living through). So, she stayed away. Although I now know it's not true, Claire's lack of interest ushered in feelings of rejection and abandonment. It was easy to conclude she didn't care - like she had *never really* cared at all.

While my world was spinning and collapsing all at the same time, it seemed I had lost the woman who had helped me keep it structured and on track. Claire had trusted me with her children, let me do my laundry in her machine, eat Thanksgiving dinner at her table and prayed me through other hardships. Now, she didn't want to hear from me. She had vanished. I had heard the ones who are closest to you are the ones who have the power to hurt you the most, and this terrible truth was finally told to me.

"When your best friend doesn't show up to your baby shower" were painful words to write - but it was *excruciating* to live. Not only was my confidant not there to confide in and be a shoulder to cry on when my world was falling apart, she chose not to be there to celebrate the one beacon of light shining through the dark cloud that was hovering over me. Again, it felt like Claire was drawing a line of allegiance in the sand. I wanted her there, and I kept wishing she'd walk through the door with a gift in hand and a smile on her face, but she never showed. I would have loved her warm embrace, but instead I felt her cold shoulder. I needed her to be an umbrella to shield me from the blast that the black cloud created. I also needed her to share in my joy at that time. But, she didn't come to shower me with blessing. Instead, she left me out in the rain.

How ever you've been hurt by the women in your lives, the pain is real and deep. Chances are, if you've loved, you've been wounded. And, chances are, healing won't happen overnight. I'd like to say that my healing and full restoration was quick. It wasn't. I wanted to hold on tight. I wanted to force my feelings on her. I wanted her to understand how wrong she was, though she thought she was doing the right thing. It seemed like an impossibility that we could ever get back to where we were. It all felt....exactly how Satan wanted it to be.

Just as the "weird sisters" in Shakespeare's "Macbeth" represent evil, chaos and impending doom, you can be certain that unforgiveness represents the same. Yet, forgiving our offender, the one who has inflicted pain and burrowed it deep in our hearts, is seemingly impossible. I am reminded though, of a truth buried even deeper in my heart, which tells me that with God, *all* things are possible.

A Necessary Evil

Let's talk about our enemy for just a moment. Though, a moment is all I want to give him. You have to understand one thing. Your enemy is not the person who inflicted that pain of offense you're feeling. Your enemy is the one who inflicts *all* pain. And it is not just possible, but certainly probable that he is working overtime behind the scenes to ensure that you hold on to every weighty ounce of that pain for a very long time. It is definite that he is against you.

In her book, *Fervent*, Priscilla Shirer convinces me once again that Satan isn't just a metaphor, but a very real enemy with a name, and he is up to no good in my relationships. He wants all of us to suffer as often as possible.

She writes, "*If I were your enemy, I'd use every opportunity to bring old wounds to mind, as well as the people, events and circumstances that caused them. I'd try to ensure that your heart was hardened with anger and bitterness. Shackled through unforgiveness".*

Friends, this is exactly how the oppressor keeps us bound.

Our enemy encourages us to keep suffering by lobbying us to not forgive. We get tied up in ropes of bitterness when we believe there is power in holding on. He wants us to promote our "rights" and protect our own "dignity" because he knows we hold onto the suffering at the same time - and he *loves* when we suffer.

We have believed a lie about the benefit of a grudge, presuming we are stronger if we hold on, as if relationships are a game of "Tug of War". Satan lied when he said you win when you tighten your grip until your knuckles turn white. He lied when he said there will be no more war within you once you've yanked your opponent into the pit. He knows that with forgiveness comes freedom and he, instead, wants you bound. Revenge never produces peace.

Now, enough of The Father of Lies. Enough of holding on.

The Truth About Letting Go

The Bible uses numerous Greek words to talk about forgiveness, which should not surprise any of us since salvation is not possible without it! Two of the words have had a profound impact on me. The first is *Charizomai*, which means "to give grace." It is a choice of the heart to not hold grudges, not hold another's actions against them and to view them with compassion rather than judgment. Andy Stanley says when we have forgiven we say in our hearts about the offender, "You don't owe me." This is never easy to do but very freeing. The other Greek word is *Aphiemi*, which literally means "to send away." The word is commonly translated "to let go" which gives interesting insight into the process of forgiveness.

Too many times, when we have been wronged, we fortuitously want to hold on. By mistake, we grip tight to the things that keep us bound in grief. We lock memories up inside our minds, hoping that replaying them will somehow heal them. We clamp our grips onto our right to be right until they are calloused. We think that holding on will make us feel better and be better. The reality is that *letting go* heals the wounds.

In the game "Tug of War", the people who "let go" are rendered the losers and concluded to be the weaker ones. But in the game of life - abundant life - "letting go" actually reveals great strength and fortitude. I don't know about you, but I just don't have this kind of strength on my own. I need "the God of the Impossible" to help me loosen my grip.

The God of the Impossible let go. He let go of His right to nail us for our sins against Him, providing us a way out at great cost to Himself. He let go of His dignity, so that His hands could be spread wide and nailed to a cross. His forgiveness is what gives us strength and reason to forgive our debtors. My corresponding *Get Along Guide* Bible Study gives insights into how I managed the strength to "let go", and how *you* can too. It will offer you four practical points that will lead you to full forgiveness, and hopefully, restoration with your offender.

He never said it would be easy (in fact, you must be tough as nails), but He said to do it - to let go. He did the impossible so that we could too.

So, when the caldron of unforgiveness is burning and bubbling within, let "The God of the Impossible" tug at your heart, free your grip and be the cool, healing balm to that burn. When the enemy is dancing on every wound, reminding you of all that's been done to you, take the advice of Priscilla Shirer, and...

"Forgive anyway. Not because it's easy but because your enemy gets exactly what he wants from you otherwise. Forgive anyway. Not lightly and quickly but ferociously and fervently. Not only for the other person but mostly for you - so you can be free and full and whole and complete."

Relational Reasons to Forgive

Thankfully, I walked the path of forgiveness and experienced a face to face, heartfelt apology from my offender. Even more wonderful, Claire and me have continued our relationship and we love each other as dearly as we once did. It has been beautiful. That doesn't mean my life was not weighed down by my ugly unforgiveness. As you read earlier, it consumed every part of me and tainted my outlook on people in general. I became cynical and wondered if I could trust again. Unforgiveness doesn't just affect our relationship with our offender. It touches every area of our lives and everyone we are surrounded by. Take these consequences into consideration:

1) Your relationship with your offender will suffer. This is an obvious one when it comes to larger offenses, but if we hold on to even the petty stuff, it will wedge itself between even the best of friends. Sometimes we do not have a relationship with our offender, but most of the time we do - and they are often the ones we are closest to. I am deeply loyal to the friends and family members who have shown me grace when I've wronged them. We must do the same. If we do not fully let go of the big and the small stuff, even your closest relationships will suffer and eventually dissolve.

2) Your relationships with others will be affected. A very strong and mature friend of mine shared a time she had to overcome holding onto a grudge. She needed to forgive a sister-in-law for not repaying her and her husband a loan. Not only did she battle ill feelings towards her sister-in-law, but it affected her at family gatherings. Although she tried to conceal it, her disdain noticeably seeped out of her causing tension to fill the air. Family members who had absolutely no involvement, or even awareness of the matter, began to feel that tension. Gatherings which were normally lighthearted and fun for everyone, became awkward and strained. You will find the same could happen to you. Eventually it won't just be you who must suffer from and cope with your bitterness. You will pass that burden on to the ones who you do want to be in your life.

3) You will be tormented. When I was having trouble forgiving, I would sweat and stew when I should have been conked out in a glorious state of slumber. And, when I was supposed to be awake, I just wanted to be put out of my misery. My head ached, my teeth clenched, my chest was tight. My unforgiveness touched every area of my life - the way I viewed other people (cynically), the prayers (or lack of) that I sent up to God, and my entire attitude and countenance throughout my day. Chronic unforgiveness affects more than just your mood. It can cause sleeplessness, stress and headaches, anxiety and more - I now know this to be true.

My husband's friend who is educated in drug therapy and emotional/mental illness explained to me that patterns of thought can physically forge lines and restructure the pattern of our brain. If we continually think negative thoughts, we are literally messing with our minds! And, our bodies are greatly affected by what is going on in our mind. Brace yourself for these alarming reports from doctors who have studied this issue:

According to Dr. Steven Standiford, chief of surgery at the Cancer Treatment Centers of America, *"Unforgiveness is classified in medical books as a disease. Refusing to forgive makes people sick and keeps them that way."*[19]

In her book *What Your Future Holds And What You Can Do To Change It*, Deborah Finley explains the toll unforgiveness will take on our bodies:

> *"Unforgiveness distresses your muscular-skeletal system by increasing forehead muscle tension, thereby producing headaches, and by also producing other symptoms: stomach aches, joint pain/aches,*

dizziness and tiredness...your digestion is impaired. And while unforgiveness may not be the sole cause of all of them, it increases your vulnerability to them. It can set the scene for them, and it can delay or even prevent your recovery...people who refuse to forgive hurt themselves.

Bitter people are no fun to be around. They can't sleep. Ulcers line their stomach. They see the negative in every situation because their life is filled with these feelings of resentment and anger. People who are unwilling to forgive may feel they are punishing the other person but the only person paying the price is themselves. "[20]

No need for me to say anything more. Deborah's words are convincing enough! We need to make forgiveness a priority!

4) Your relationship with God will be stunted. As if our human relationships being negatively affected isn't daunting enough, our unforgiveness will certainly affect our spiritual relationship with God our Father as well. Unforgiveness leads to the pathway of a hardened heart. It clogs the arteries to Him. When we dig our heels in and choose not to forgive, we grieve the one who's forgiven us. But, when our hearts are soft, and teachable, we are able to walk down the path to forgiveness. The issue is not as much about our sin (because it is inevitable) as it is about the posture of our heart. Think of King David and the sin that entangled him. He pursued actions that would put citizens in jail - and yet, he was called "a man after God's own heart". Why? He humbled himself and asked God to search his heart to find the wicked ways. He was begging God to help him in his areas of weakness. He wasn't without sin but he asked God to help him remove it. David had conversations with God. He was intimate with him. God craves that kind of connection with us too, but our unwillingness shuts the door. Although it takes time, if you're headed in the direction towards forgiveness, you will get there, as you stay close to God. Your mistakes will not keep you from God's love, but you won't enjoy intimacy with him when you choose to remain in sin.

Letting Go Will Help You Grow

I know what you're thinking if you are in the place where your heart is still raw. You just don't want to let her off the hook. Well, God tells us that it's our job to release and it's *His* job to take the reigns and handle the rest. Be assured, He is a grace-filled and loving God, but also a just God, and he will fight for you. You must only keep calm, hold your peace and keep silent (Exodus 14:14). Letting go will help you grow. Instead of shriveling under the weight of bitterness, you will flourish as an individual and in every one of your relationships.

"Do not be overcome by evil,
but overcome evil with good."
~ Romans 12:21

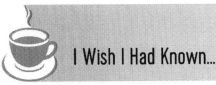

I Wish I Had Known...

...Right feelings follow right actions.

"In life, there will be countless little moments we must forgive and move on. Thankfully, there have only been a few times I've wound up in a position where I really needed to do some hardcore forgiving. I learned something with each experience and, no matter who my offender was, or to what degree the hurt, the same thing was true: those feelings of freedom that forgiveness brings *don't* come naturally.

Just like a married couple of twenty years must make a continual, conscious choice to love, we must make a concentrated effort to forgive. This means taking action. And, the best actions you can take are obeying God's word. God says to *pray* for our offender. So, that I did. That is *hard*. But, what I found, once I succumbed, is that, over time, my feelings would begin to follow my actions.

It is similar to our muscles when we exercise them. We can't feel or will them into shape - we must *do* something about it. It is the same with forgiveness. We can forge a path of forgiveness in our brains by continuing to choose to forgive. I wish I'd have known this from the start and my heart would have suffered less."

~ Danielle Macaulay

Reflective Questions

~ What situation do I need to let go of?

~ What specific actions could I take to loosen my grip?

~ If I choose to hold on to my rights as a victim, what will I gain?

We have identified the things that spoil our relationships. Now let's discover the secret ingredients that make them sweet. God is the baker - we are His sous chef. Together, we will create something wonderful.

Section 2

GOD'S RECIPE FOR RELATIONSHIP SUCCESS

CHAPTER 9
A Pinch of Patience

"No one can drive us crazy unless we give them the keys" ~ *Doug Horton*

A Thorn in My Flesh

She was a royal pain. I was convinced she had it in for me, which is why I privately nicknamed her *Thorn*. You'd never be able to peg her for it though. She had discrete manipulation, twisted compliments and secret sabotage down to a science. I found it all unwarranted. Although she concealed her disdain for me, a cold war was transpiring under the surface. As far as I was concerned, she was the embodiment of the "thorn in the flesh" Paul referred to in 2 Corinthians. If I'm truly honest, she was on my mind when I stared out my kitchen window with gritted teeth asking God, "Why can't we all just get along?!"

I wasn't prepared to *actually* receive an answer. As I gazed out the window, my mind was flooded with new thoughts, *You* **can** *get along. God is going to show you how. In fact, it's already laid out in His Word. You must be patient with her because she is fighting the same battle you did.* You see, I remember when my insecurity, jealousy, envy, propensity to compete and dedication to compare myself to another woman made my inner disposition as prickly as a thorn too.

I Hate Her

Grace was everything lovely, a flower adding life and beauty to her surroundings. Like the antique filled rooms of her home, she was cultured, interesting and pristine. Each corner of her personality invited you in and enticed you to discover more, like the stately staircase in her welcoming front entryway. Grace was as charming as her china collection and her temperament was as put together as her four course dinners. The features of her face were as beautiful as the curves of her clawfoot tub.

Grace welcomed me into her stunning home and life with open arms, making it clear she was there for me as she lavished me with the most generous and thoughtful gifts. She was the most lovely and godly woman I'd ever crossed paths with. Everyone loved her – and why wouldn't they?

But, I *hated* her.
Ouch. Did I really just admit that in print?

I did. I loathed her for no sensible reason. Why on God's green Earth did I harbor such ill-will toward her? I was drawn to this woman, and loved everything about her, except her. I wished I was more like her - and hated that I wasn't. Her life was everything I dreamed of, but it wasn't mine.

A young girl with a humble upbringing, I felt inadequate and insecure. I was threatened by this seemingly perfect woman. I wondered if my soon to be husband would prefer someone like her over me. I certainly didn't have Egyptian cotton. I wasn't sure I knew what "organic" even meant. And, I couldn't cook worth beans!

Coming from a single parent, shoestring budget home, my meals were the boxed or canned food sale of the week. The beige walls in our house remained that way because there simply was no extra money, while she was living in color. I fantasized about living a life like hers and I feared this was Dan's desire as well. I resented that my life felt... beige.

I compared everything. I stacked up my failures and deficiencies against her strengths creating a game I couldn't win. It turned me into someone I detested, and at times, someone who was unattractive to Dan. My prickles were engulfing my petals.

Thorn Removal

The precise moment when I "had it up to here" with this pesky person I call "Thorn," God swooped in. He lovingly, yet sternly, reminded me of my own battle years before. The truth dug deep like a double-edged sword but it allowed me to identify with this burdensome woman. She suddenly became an ally who was warring within rather than my enemy. My heart softened as I saw me in her. I began to recognize someone who was fragile and broken, not just my offender. I, too, had known what it was like to struggle with another woman, to not want anything to do with her, and yet wish to *be* her all at the same time. The way I handled it looked different but the pain was the same. God gave me the ability to identify with her by presenting me with pangs from my past. This was step one in the thorn removal.

Now, "Thorn" wasn't fully extracted yet. She was not a quick fix. You see, the key to proper thorn removal is *patience*. We must not be tempted to use force which induces pain and can drive the embedded irritation deeper. A soothing, healing balm which gently releases the source of the sting is a superior method. After all, that "splinter" is your sister. So, proceed with care.

Removing the Plank and Releasing Stones

In order to fully remove the thorns from our flesh, we must face our tendency to judge the sin of another. Judging other women will always affect our patience levels. It is easy to become impatient with the speck in her eye, all while having a two-by-four in our own. Jesus warns us to be careful not to criticize others' failings because we are all flawed (Matthew 7:5). We are often blind to our faults, so it is important to allow God's word to remove the blinders and accept that our faults simply look *different*. Thankfully, we have been forgiven of those flaws and offenses.

> *"Make allowance for (her) faults. Forgive (her) when (she) offends you. Remember that I forgave you, so forgive her. Clothe yourself with love for (her) and that will bind you together with (her). Let my peace rule your heart. You are part of my body and I want you to live at peace with (her). And always be thankful"*

~ Colossians 3:13-15 (NLT)

Colossians 3 is designed to take on human form. It is not a metaphor or an inspirational thought. It is an active response to the grace that's already been extended to us. When we intentionally make allowance for one another in our day to day lives, we will experience peace within our own hearts and with each other.

When we withdraw our judgement, we will have the ability to release our stones. You may recall a very sinful woman who Jesus had every right to punish. What would He do? When pressed by the people who were ready to stone the woman, Jesus offered the crowd this proposal:

> *"Let any one of you who is without sin
> cast the first stone." ~ John 8:7*

Ladies, aren't you thankful that The Lord has been endlessly patient with you? He has resolved the need to punish us for our wrong attitudes and behaviors. Instead He graciously provides new mercies every day with an endless parade of patience.

So, when you are becoming exasperated, recall the ones *you* have exasperated. Remember that you are not without rough edges and realize the patience that has been provided to you.

Finally, always be thankful.

Be Thankful for What?!

Paul seems to take a sharp left turn in his letter to the church in Colossians 3:15. He groups his statements about extending forgiveness, love, peace and ultimately patience to others with counsel to remain in a constant state of thankfulness. Wait - does that include being thankful for the thorn in our flesh? Who on Earth gives praise to God for a woman who has decided to crawl under our skin? *Of course* no one would welcome that. Well, what are we to be thankful for then?

For starters, that thorn is a continual reminder of our need for God. When we have need to be patient with others, it can serve as a reminder of all that Christ has done for us and it will make us more like Him - our ultimate goal. As she digs in, she propels us to lean into Him. An opportunity to extend grace and patience is also an opportunity to share God's great love. Our willingness to be patient will help the women around us experience the power of the Holy Spirit. After all, the fruit, or evidence, of His Spirit is *patience*.

Thanks be to God for all the times he's swept my mistakes under His rug of grace and kept the corners from curling up so no one can catch a glimpse! If she is still testing your patience, remember all your mess hiding beneath the surface that His grace has covered over a multitude of times. Remember, then give thanks. This will give you His eyes and His heart for her.

Thank you, God, that when we do things Your way, see others how You see them and treat them how You treat us,

Your peace will rule our hearts and our relationships.

> *"Be always humble, gentle and patient. Show your*
> *love by being tolerant with one another."*
> *~ Ephesians 4:2*

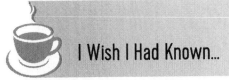

I Wish I Had Known...

...That patience trumps passion.

"In any relationship, there is a "honeymoon phase". We all get along with those who've yet to step on our toes or challenge us in any way. It is easy to think that a new friend is "better" than what's familiar to you - you haven't locked horns or crossed swords. You don't know their past, or all their baggage and idiosyncrasies.

I used to love meeting new friends, and the promise it provided. But, what I cherish now are the friendships that have endured. I am most loyal to the ones who've carried me through tough seasons. I run to those women for prayer and guidance. I think of them most fondly. And, I see now that it is worth being patient and working through difficulties, because the grass is not greener on the other side - it is greener where it is watered.

Be patient, and fight for the relationships that are worth keeping. Don't move on so quickly. Passion fades, but patience fortifies."

~ Danielle Macaulay

 Reflective Questions

- Who in my life can take on the "human form" of Colossians 3:13-15?

- Who should I be "making an allowance for"?

- Recall a time that others have made allowances for my "prickly" behavior.

CHAPTER 10
A Cup of Confession

"No one has ever choked to death from swallowing her pride. If you've done wrong, admit it"
~ Donna Kretch

Clearing the Air

Earlier we learned that misunderstandings are cause for turbulence in relationships. Often, we act awkwardly or even retract from people we have misread, or if there's unfinished business. This can crash land us into conflict as we reciprocate negative vibes. So many of us are at unnecessary odds because we aren't communicating effectively. One of the best ways to avoid lingering misunderstanding (which evolves into lingering offense) is to get things out in the open, share our honest feelings in a godly way, and clear the air. Another necessary part of "clearing the air" in a relationship is to confess our sin and pray for one another. It is nearly impossible to hold on to an offense when we bare our hearts, confess and pray.

Get the Junk Out of Your Trunk

No, I'm not talking about an intense gluteus maximus

workout. I am referring to the painful exercise of confession. Whether it means admitting to an intentional backstab, a simple slip of the tongue, or harboring negative feelings, confession is an integral ingredient of a healthy friendship. If we dance with anyone long enough, we will eventually step on their toes. It's bound to happen. When we do, we must be willing to admit to the misstep and repair what needs mending in order to continue the dance.

There is good news about bringing our sin to light. When we reveal the improper choices we made yesterday, we shed light on our maturity today. This makes confession a little less scary, doesn't it? We cannot change our past but we can certainly repent and learn from it. When we do regular junk removal, our conscience and our relationships will be lighter and less bogged down by any clutter we are hiding. We will discover unexpected freedom, intimacy and loyalty.

Matthew 18:15 tells us how to do this well:

> *"If another believer sins against you, go privately and point out the offense. If the other person listens and confesses it, you have won that person back."*

Confessing our wrong behaviors or attitudes is one of the hardest, but most powerful, choices in life.

Sorry is for the Strong

When researching this topic, I came across a couple of silly quotes:

"Never say sorry - it's a sign of weakness."
~ John Wayne.

"Love means never having to say you're sorry".
~ Erich Segal

Wait - WHAT?! Stop right there. This goes to show you can't trust everything you read. Sorry, Mr. Wayne, but admitting that you were wrong is an act of strength and bravery! Sorry Mr. Segal, but one of the best ways to keep love alive is to ask forgiveness, whether it be from a spouse, a friend and even our kids. Saying "I'm sorry" is the super glue that puts the pieces of a relationship back together. I don't know if you've ever super glued anything together, but that stuff is near Herculean!

The most effective apologies are accompanied by changed behavior. Repentance is more than remorse - it is more of a metamorphosis.

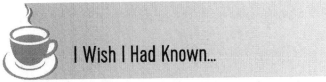

I Wish I Had Known...

...What was on the other side of my confession

I wish, when I was in the middle of the mess, I could have seen what was waiting for me on the other side of my confession. It is all so wonderful. I would have been quicker to act.

I knew the guile I was harboring in my heart towards "Grace" needed to be confessed. It was stunting and poisonous, as bitter roots wove their way around gripping every part of me. I needed to bring it into the light. I first confessed to a mentor of mine. I told her every filthy thing. I was met with understanding and compassion. My mentor prayed with me, encouraged me, but did not let me off the hook. We both agreed I needed to confess to "Grace"

So, I swallowed my pride and wrote a letter. I then followed up with a face to face conversation. Man was that hard! I cringed as I confessed, anticipating her possible rejection. Yet, she embraced me with exceedingly more mercy and love than I ever deserved. I was served grace, not just on a serving tray, but on a royal platter.

That confession ushered in full on heart remodeling and revolution. Slowly, but surely, as I determined to pray for "Grace" and practice gratitude, my attitude shifted away from envy, self-pity and insecurity. Forced prayers became genuine ones. Then, something funny happened. Grace and I began praying together. And before I knew it, I no longer viewed her as my competition. She became like a sister, someone I looked up to and was inspired by. In fact, I actually liked myself better when I was around her. Her admirable qualities began rubbing off on me and I was glad about that.

If I had not confessed, I may still be harboring hate towards her and towards myself. I am so thankful I decided to bring my darkness into the light.

That confession changed everything.

"Grace" and I have been prayer partners for well over a decade now. She has prayed me through the darkest seasons of my life. She's guided and encouraged me as a wife and mother. She has blessed me beyond what I could ever repay her. I can't even imagine my life without her in it. She is my mentor, faithful friend and soul sister. And, I'll tell you - serving trays come in handy. I have since learned that too. She is a treasure - a treasure that my sin had buried but my confession uprooted.

Pray Together to Stay Together

There is power in numbers and we are strong when we include the Lord in all of our relationships. He will help us admit our wrongdoing, fix our problem areas and keep our relationships intact.

"Though one may be overpowered, two can defend themselves. A cord of three strands is not quickly broken." ~ Ecclesiastes 4:12

Married couples stay intact and thrive when they pray together. Prayer is oxygen for marriage. Couples who pray together have a divorce rate of 1 in 10,000. That sure beats the statistics of 1 in 2 couples divorcing in America by a long shot (Relationship Rescue, Dr. Phil).[7] Just as a husband and wife need prayer in their relationship, prayer can prevent female friendships from flatlining too! Nothings says you care for someone like when you take the time to intercede for them. And, it's hard to stay mad at anyone when you are genuinely praying with their best interest in mind. God changes our minds when we pray. Prayer mends broken thoughts, broken hearts and broken relationships. When you pray with a friend, you weave your hearts together in a strong bond that creates a catalyst of change.

So You May Be Healed

James tells us to confess our sins to one another and pray for each other for very good reason...so that we may be healed. Too many of us are wandering around beat up, bruised and broken over things we've said or done poorly, or because of another woman's wrongdoing. If that's you, don't you want to make amends?

There's no Time Like the Present

Confession is a gift. It is a present both to the woman you're confessing to and to yourself. If you have waited to confess, you may think there's no point to deliver it because it is like offering a wilted flower or stale piece of cake. But I promise you, no matter how long you've had unfinished business to deal with, there is no time like the present.

There have been several times throughout my life I've given an overdue apology, or have been blessed by one. In every case, when done earnestly, it should be met with gratitude and grace.

There was one girl whose apology to me was eight years in the making. She had treated me unfairly and unkindly when she was much younger, still growing wings of maturity. Although she frustrated me at the time, I did my best to be gracious with her. I completely understood. Years passed. I harbored no resentment towards her and nearly forgot about her teenage attitude towards me.

The next part of this story should happen so much more often. Now, a married adult, my offender sought me out, even though our lives had moved on. She humbly asked for my forgiveness and apologized for how she had treated me long ago. I was floored and appreciative that she would do that. In my mind it was not necessary, but for her it was. It was relieving and freeing for her. While it was "water under the bridge" for me, the apology became a bridge that connected us and created a friendship.

Ladies, it's not too late! Dismiss the thoughts that tell you there is no point for an apology because it seems that she, or you, have moved on. No matter how long it's been, if you confess your sin and genuinely ask forgiveness, God will honor your act of courage. So, don't wait any longer. Clearing the air and getting the junk out of your trunk will make you breathe easier, feel lighter and your relationships will be stronger for it.

*Therefore confess your sins to each other and pray
for each other so that you may be healed.*
~ James 5:16

Reflective Questions

~ What could my relationship with the individual I have wronged look like if I braved a confession, apology or an attempt at making amends?

~ What is holding you back today from approaching someone who has wronged you or whom you have wronged?

CHAPTER 11
An Ounce of Openness and a Teaspoon of Truth

"We will never feel loved until we drop the act, until we're willing to show our true selves to the people around us." ~ Donald Miller, Scary Close

Big and Buried Burdens

Our burdens are big. Overwhelming, and almost too much to bear at times. And yet, when people ask us how we're doing, we are always..."*Great!*"

We do whatever we can to cover up depression, anxiety, fear and habitual sin like a pimple on prom day. Our husband's character flaws, our children's bad behavior and our parent's dysfunction can never ever be found out. And, don't even think about answering the door to a friend if you're in your old bleach stained pregnancy yoga pants. We do too much of life covered up and closed off.

Air Your Dirty Laundry

There's something relieving and refreshing when

someone else says "me too!" It forms instant connection and greater intimacy which is worlds better than a bunch of "oohs and ahhs". In order to hear "me too", we must first be willing to divulge. I'm not talking about letting it all hang out on social media - no one wants that. Virtual rubbernecking only leads to emotional crash. We simply need to be more willing to be *vulnerable* and *real* with one another. It means we need to take our defenses down and be willing to "air some of our dirty laundry"...

Baseball season is always busy and this year my eldest will be playing in two leagues. Many days and nights we will be at the diamond, on top of all the other chaos the end of the school year brings. We absolutely love cheering Keaton on, but I tell ya, making sure his dirty, stanky (yes, I said *stanky*) uniform is clean several times a week isn't exactly on the top of my to do list. Sometimes chores literally get shoved to the bottom of the pile. His uniform was one of them.

One hectic Tuesday night, as we rushed around to shove food into our mouth and gather his equipment, I realized I had failed to wash his uniform. I found it in a damp, wrinkled heap under a few wet towels in the laundry room. I quickly whipped it in the dryer in a vain attempt to freshen it up, hoping no one would be the wiser. As I handed the uniform to an annoyed 9-year-old, he reminded me that major league players don't go on the field with a dirty, wrinkled uniform, so neither should he. This was the only time he'd ever cared an iota about having clean clothes. I sighed a big breath of frustration and we proceeded to the game.

When we arrived, I casually chit chatted with the other

moms, pretending I wasn't stressed and feeling like a failure. Out of the glorious nowhere, it seemed, I heard my friend Cindy begin to confess that it had been a busy day... and guess what - *she had pulled her son's uniform directly out of the hamper for the game.* She had *"failed"* too. As my mouth dropped in disbelief and my eyes bugged out of my head, the seemingly calm cool and collected lady to my left became a bit unraveled and piped up "me too!" I chimed in with "You're kidding! Me too!" We all laughed and, in the words of my five year old, felt a "trillion, million, dillion, ba-jillion" times better.

This woman's confession miraculously turned my sigh of frustration and defeat into one of relief. I imagine it was the same for the other mom as well. Airing our "dirty laundry" to each other instantaneously connected us. We went from feeling like a solitary failure to bonding and banding together.

This is what baring and sharing does.

Dare to Share

You see, we become much more fused together when we bravely share our burdens. If you are tempted to keep all your "dirty laundry" hidden, remember there's also a pile your neighbor is trying to conceal. She has disappointments and deficiencies, inadequacies and areas of insufficiency too. The circumstances aren't as rosy as they seem. There is a weight on her shoulders that you can help heave off of her. And, she can rescue you too - but only when you're willing to *share* your burdens. This might mean that she may catch a whiff of that dirty laundry. I promise you though, the sweet aroma of true, authentic friendship overpowers the stench we feel we need to mask.

Lighten her Load

I have rarely seen a stronger force than when a group of people unite over a struggle. As we air that dirty laundry of ours, we unite beautifully. When we walk through turmoil, besides prayer, there is nothing more powerful and transformative than a "support group". I have personally benefited from others coming alongside me to lighten my load during a time of hardship. I know I am not the only one. Whether we are walking through cancer, divorce or a wayward child, if we can share it, we can get through it much easier together. Community is cardinal and crucial.

It is hard to reveal our flaws and share our problems, but airing that dirty laundry and lightening the load allows others to encourage and build us up. It also gives them the opportunity to help us become more like Christ because when we mask our imperfections, we also cover our sin. On the other hand, when we show others who we really truly are - taking off the mask and getting scary close - our weaknesses are revealed.

Believe me or not, this is a *good* thing.

So, I dare you to bare. Bare it all to your trusted ones. Show them all of you. The real you. Your relationship with Christ will grow stronger, your friendships will deepen and your burdens will be lifted.

The Highlight Reel Ain't Real

This epidemic of keeping our burdens buried is at an all time high because of......you guessed it - *social media*. I am convinced. We are in each other's lives virtually more than ever, but not actually in them *for real*. What we see on social media *isn't* fully genuine so it causes our daily, weighed down selves to retract. More than ever, we feel our problems are out of the ordinary because we aren't hearing about other's real-life problems, we're only seeing filtered snippets of their successes. We conclude we must be the freaks who can't keep it together. So, we don't dare admit that our days aren't sugar and spice and everything nice. Let me remind you of this, and I'll repeat it until I'm blue in the face: *the highlight reel ain't real.*

It is funny who we call "friends" these days. A "friend" can be anyone from our hairdresser to our housekeeper. I just checked my Facebook profile page. According to that, I have 1,735 "friends". I am willing to bet that I have never met at least half of those friends in person. And some friends who actually *genuinely* know me the most aren't on Facebook. Go figure.

Let's not limit our social media reporting to touting our successes only. Galatians 6:2 challenges us to share our burdens with one another also. Bragging and boasting may impress a few, but will keep most others at bay. Only proclaiming your struggles will eventually become exhausting. But, sharing a balance of our successes and struggles will reveal our real selves, which always promotes unity. In *Scary*

109

Close, Donald Miller sets things straight:

> *"It's true, people are attracted to intelligence and strength and even money, but attraction isn't intimacy. What attracts us doesn't always connect us."*[8]

So, the question I pose to you is, would you rather be envied, or truly loved? What do you need more - admiration or intimacy? Will you save face, or let your guard down and live face to face?

So, what is a real friend? I'll tell you again - it's not a "reel" friend..

True Friendship

I asked women to describe characteristics of the BEST friends they've ever had. These were the answers I got:

> *"A genuine friend is someone who will tell you the truth. Not just what you want to hear".*

> *"Real friends don't offer lip service, but the truth in love".*

> *"They are willing to say the tough things but in a gentle way."*

> *"My best friends poke me a little to be my best self".*

> *"My dear friends are the ones who help me grow".*

*"They are understanding, yet able to encourage you
to do the best thing without judging you."*

*"They are honest and willing to tell me the truth in a
loving, but upfront way so I could grow."*

Hmm - speaks the truth in love, available, loyal, nonjudgmental, there to listen, honest, trustworthy - that sums up my most genuine relationships as well. Unfortunately, not a single one of those characteristics can be properly lived out via the internet. By all means, connect with your friends on social media. Follow their Instagram pics and have fun with them on Snapchat. But, don't leave the chats to that.

When it comes to building and maintaining genuine relationships, we know that social media falls short. It is more beneficial to eat freshly squeezed orange juice than it is to pop a vitamin C pill. Likewise, it is healthier to enjoy the benefits of face to face relationship than it is to converse through a screen. Enjoy the *real* thing!

Genuine Affection

Of course we all want genuine friendship as opposed to virtual or superficial ones. So, what does that look like?

God tells us to love with *"genuine affection"*. Romans 12:9, 10 says "Don't just pretend to love others. Really love them...love each other with *genuine* affection."

The definition of Genuine is *"Truly what something is said* to be. *Authentic, sincere and bona fide"*. I want that to be said of me and I am sure you do too. No one likes a fake. We can all sniff one out. Being complimented insincerely or ingenuinely or blown off can leave us frustrated at best. What then, does loving others with "genuine affection" practically look like? Are we living up to who we *think* we are, or are we disingenuous and put on? How do we know we are *really* loving others so that it is beneficial for them and not just filling our own needs?

Truth Telling

Of course, we women want friends with whom we can laugh, party, or look good with, but what we highly value are those who will encourage us and challenge us to be a better version of ourselves. We may not see it at the time, but what we all value in friendship is someone who is *open* and *real* with us to help us grow. A genuine friend is a truth telling friend - one who is honest about themselves and compassionately courageous with us.

Now, we must earn the right to be a truth teller by building trust with one another. It is not a given that you can trust everyone you meet. Please don't confuse genuine friends with judgmental friends. Some people like to share their opinions like a communicable disease. Some of you have had "fake friends" mistreat you for so long that it has become your norm. A frog would never jump into a boiling pot of water, but leave it in a tepid one that you gradually bring to a boil, and they'll be cooked before they realize! To keep you from being burned, here are some characteristics of fake friends, and of real ones.

Fake Friends vs Real Friends

A fake friend judges you and is conditional.
A real friend loves you when you aren't being lovable.

A fake friend doesn't return any of your messages and is always too busy for you.
A real friend reaches out and makes time for you.

A fake friend only cares about what they have to offer.
A real friend listens.

A fake friend bad mouths you.
A real friend builds you up.

A fake friend protects their reputation over the relationship.
A real friend defends you when you need protecting.

A fake friend's promises are hollow.
A real friend comes through for you.

A fake friend doesn't say I'm sorry.
A real friend owns up to their mistakes.

A fake friend takes advantage of you.
A real friend gives without expecting something in return.

A fake friend has their best interest in mind.
A real friend has your best interest in mind.

So, are you open? Are you real? If not, I challenge you to drop the act in order to gain the most intimate and rewarding friendships you've had yet.

"Genuine kindness doesn't have ulterior motives"
~ Zero Dean

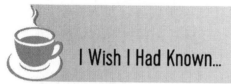

I Wish I Had Known...

...That honesty (about yourself) is the best policy

"It's easy to believe that denying parts of our real self and cherry-picking our best qualities to reveal to others is a fine course of action. In fact, it just makes us weird.

Eleanor Roosevelt said:

"You have to be honest with yourself. You must try to understand truthfully what makes you do things or feel things. Until you have been able to face the truth about yourself you cannot be really sympathetic or understanding in regard to what happens to other people. But it takes courage to face yourself and acknowledge what motivates you in the things you do."

If we choose to only see ourselves in the best light then we settle into a kind of darkness, really. We reside in a foggy existence that hides us from ourselves and from others. As a result, no one can accept us for who we *really* are.

Ultimately, not being truthful with ourselves stunts/hinders our relationship with God as well as with others. We must be honest no matter what the consequences are. James 5:16 explains that confession leads to healing. John 8:32 says the truth of Jesus will set us free from sin. If we honestly say, *"I'm broken,"* we have the chance to change. If we say, *"There's nothing wrong, I've got it, I don't need help,"* then nothing can be fixed - though God in his grace may eventually confront us: *"Why are you naked?"* We continue down the road of not being fixed and of not being known—and that's a long, lonely road.

Really, at the heart of this conundrum is pride. Pride is one of the most toxic motivations of all because it puts us in a holding pattern of denial. It is the opposite of honesty so it will always be incredibly stunting.

Each time we're confronted with the opportunity for honesty we face a fork in the road. We can head farther down the path of self-delusion, immaturity and isolation or we can steer toward transformation, maturity, and intimacy. If we choose to face our real motivations and faults, we may be more overwhelmed by the love, acceptance and encouragement of others than we were by our pride and fear. I wish I'd have grasped how honesty with myself (and, therefore others) would have benefited me earlier in my life."

~ Karen Root

Reflective Questions

~ What areas about myself do my friends truly know me? What parts have I kept hidden?

~ How has social media distorted my view of other women?

~ What burdens have I tried to carry on my own?

~ Who are my go-to "safe" women with whom I can share my burdens?

CHAPTER 12
A Smidgen of Service and a Litre of Love

"Only a life worth living for others is worth living."
~ Albert Einstein

Make her Comfortable

Has there ever been a time when you can sense another woman struggles to be around you? Maybe she feels inadequate or insecure in your presence. Maybe *she's* jealous of you. She might wish she could be just like you, or at least have what you have.

Let me ask you another question: Do you like that feeling? Do you *enjoy* knowing others feel they are less than you? It's flattering to know you are envied but, as I say in the previous chapter of this book, it is not better to be envied than truly loved - not even close. And, it is certainly not better to be self-serving. Life is best when we put the feelings and needs of others above ourselves. We must strive to make women feel comfortable around us and avoid "tripping another woman's insecurity switch", as Beth Moore calls it (So Long Insecurity). The Apostle Paul instructs us to...

"Decide instead to live in such a way that you will not cause another believer to stumble and fall".
~ Romans 14:13

Rocks and a Recipe for Relational Disaster

I cringe as I remember a time I whipped up a recipe for relational disaster. I didn't care about serving another woman's needs and I actually enjoyed tripping her insecurity switch. I preferred the praise of others over making another woman feel comfortable around me.

The year I got engaged (at the tender age of 19), I picked up a retail job for extra money to pay for the wedding. I worked at a glamorous lingerie store (handy, I know). One of my favorite parts of the job was folding the delicate silks and laces into boxes with tissue and deliciously scented fragrant beads. We would tie each package with ribbon and seal it with a beautifully embossed sticker. This process would take place at a dramatically lit counter, with the customer watching our fingers do the magic.

It became a daily joy for me to wrap these beautiful gifts under the lights. While my fingers were doing the work, I'd often be complimented on my engagement ring, which would sparkle radiantly under the bright lights. It was fun to see the stone glimmer with every motion. Part of the fun in the project was the customers regularly taking note of my rock.

One of my coworkers had also become engaged. She was more subdued in nature than me, as was the size of her ring. I didn't hear much from her about her ring, her engagement or her romance - most likely because I never asked. On the other hand, she repeatedly heard *all* about mine. It occurred to me one day that this girl, who I'm sure must have been equally excited about her engagement, was caught in a one-sided conversation that only included listening to her self-centered coworker go on and on. At best, her eyes were rolling at me and, at worst, I made her feel insignificant. Either way, needless to say, we weren't very good friends. You can't be good friends with someone who makes you feel like you come up short.

Sadly, this realization did not stop me from flaunting my ring. I welcomed the attention, even in the presence of my co worker. I didn't mind that I was the one in the spotlight, and even worse, I didn't mind that she was in my shadow.

Keep Your Rock In Your Pocket

With a few more years of maturity under my belt, I now know what I should have done. *I should have kept my hand in my pocket.* I should have accepted a compliment if it came my way and then swiftly moved on. I should have asked her about her romance and pivoted the spotlight onto her so she could shine. I should have praised her in front of others. Oh, how I wish I could turn back time! I wish my 19 year-old self was more of a cheerleader and less of a glory hog.

Now, I thoroughly enjoy giving a compliment to someone

I feel is in need of one. I've discovered there's even more joy and satisfaction that comes with verbalizing the value of others. It truly is better to give than receive, especially when giving compliments. So, let's be generous, selfless and humble. Let's keep our "rocks in our pocket" and let others shine.

Recipe for Relational Success

There's some ingredients (or, a few "findings", as my Grandma June used to say) that I've discovered go into the recipe for making other women feel at ease around you. If you are able to master these, women will find you simply irresistible! They will keep coming back for more.

#1-Be Sensitive to other women's needs and insecurities. Don't aggravate or dismiss when you know something you do or say bothers another woman. Tread lightly rather than stomping over everyone around you. Decide to "live in such a way that will not cause her to stumble," and to keep the peace as best you can. (Romans 14:13) If you know a woman struggles with her weight, don't stand in front of her and discuss how you conquered another half marathon. Or, if you know she's an insecure mother, praise what she does well and resist the urge to parent her parenting. In all we do, let's consider how we can build one another up..

#2-Be a Cheerleader - Not a "*sneer*-leader" - Do you notice that when women are succeeding, there are often naysayers close by? Women often sneer at other women who are doing well because it is difficult to fully applaud other women when we are not confident in who God created us to be. So, if you are not able to cheer on another woman, there may be something you need to alter in your heart. The good news is you build your own confidence when you pay others a compliment too. This is how we can help our heart to shift. Building others up builds us up. But, nothing good comes from attempting to stunt another woman's confidence, successes or relationships. So, be a cheerleader, and not a "*sneer-leader*". If she is shining for Jesus, let her shine! Don't try to snuff her out!

#3 - Take Yourself Lightly - Those who are selfless simply think of them self less. One way you achieve this is limiting how much you talk about yourself (preaching to myself here). Also, make fun, or make light of who you are and you will become more approachable. Other women will not feel comfortable around you if you come across too serious or as "top dog". Arrogance and a condescending attitude will repel others from you. But, humility (God confidence) is attractive to others. She will feel at ease around you when you ease up. And hey, acting like a complete and utter goofball on occasion (and not caring about how you come across) really makes things fun!

#4 - Pay Attention! When we talk about ourselves less, we make space to listen! My husband is much better at way too many things than me. One of them is his ability to listen. Over the years (and it's taken that long!), he's proven to me the benefits of truly listening to another individual. When you pay attention to another woman, you actively show her that you value her. So, put that iPhone down and stop thinking about your next thought, or what you're making for dinner that night! Just *listen*. My hubby is truly a fun, funny, interesting guy...and he has many wild stories he could tell, but I respect how he sits back and listens to others share their stories. He doesn't try to "one up" nor does he feel the need to be the center of attention. And, he jokes that it's amazing how interesting people will think you are when you *just listen to them*. Give it a try!

#5 - Give her Space. If what she really needs is to *not* be around you, allow her the space and time to approach you on her terms. And, if that's *not at all*, that's ok. Not everyone will be your friend or your fan. We can't always change how others feel about us, but often we can. Give it your best attempt to win her over, but also stay sensitive to the fact that she may be better off without you close by. We must be kind to everyone, but we don't need to force ourselves on everyone.

#6 - Be Golden. Do unto others as you would have them do unto you. (Matthew 7:12). Seems so easy, right? But, in order for us to direct our eyes to the needs of others, we must take them off ourselves. This is the quandary. At the end of the day we want our own needs to be met. We want comfort. And, we often shut the door on anything that challenges that. Too often, we turn the channel quickly when we are presented with an opportunity to give towards poverty, illness or tragedy. Or, we pray for others, but don't want to practically be the answer to their prayer. Too often, we want others to be helped, but we don't want to be the ones to offer the help if it infringes on our comfort zone. Yet, the golden rule requires *empathy* and *initiative*.

Let's look at the Message's version of the golden rule,

Matthew 7:12:

*"Here is a simple, rule of thumb guide for behavior.
Ask yourself what you want people to do for you,
then grab the initiative and do it for them. Add up
God's law and Prophets and this is what you get."*

Empathy is the essence behind the golden rule. It is the ability to understand and share the feelings of another. But, it takes *initiative* to fulfill the law, which is loving others as yourself.

You may think people who live out the Golden Rule are the more gentle, pleasant or soft among us. But, empathy isn't a warm fuzzy feeling. On the contrary - it takes a certain durability. Allowing your full self - your thoughts, will and emotions - to be focused on another's needs takes a bit of brawn to handle. Initiative calls us to sacrifice our time, talent, and yes, sometimes our dollars. It calls us into action when it's easier to stay in our seats. This is reserved for the toughest among us.

Golden Girls

A pastor I greatly respect said once *"Strong people stand up for themselves, but stronger people stand up for others."* (Kevin Shepherd)

Gold is among the rarest and most valuable of treasures. But, it is not strongest on it's own. It needs help from an outside source. It's strength increases when it is teamed up with silver, copper, platinum or other metals. It is the same with us. We have the power to come forth as gold...but only when we team up with The Lord. When we are weak, *He* is strong!

As your relationships are tested and sometimes put through the fire, ask God to help them come forth as gold. They have the best chance of doing so when we love, serve and stand up for each other. When we actively put other women's needs above our own and treat them the way we wish to be treated, we are creating a recipe for success!

> *"All of you, serve each other in humility."*
> *~ 1 Peter 5:5*

 ## I Wish I Had Known...

...It's lonely on top.

"When I was a young girl, insecurity drove my need to be on top. And often, I found myself up there. I was at the top of my class. I won awards. I scored goals. I worked to make sure I was the prettiest, most talented, most envied in the room. It felt good - momentarily.

What I realize now, though, is that striving for perfection, or at least to be better than others - well, it wards people off. It kept other girls at arms length. I may have made myself an enemy, the competition, or at least someone that other girls

124

were turned off by or felt insecure around. I wish I could turn back time so I could wipe the makeup off, let more girls in to see the "real" Danielle, be more ok with letting others shine or win, so that I wouldn't have isolated myself quite as much as I'm sure I must have.

I look back now and wonder how many parties I was excluded from, how much more intimate of friendships I could have made, or who else I wouldn't have isolated myself from if I'd have known that it's much more lonely on top."

~ Danielle Macaulay

 Reflective Questions

~ When should I have "kept my rock in my pocket"?

~ Who needs me to love, serve and stand up for them?

~ Who needs me to cheer for them?

CHAPTER 13
A Dash of Discretion

"Kind words do not cost much, but they accomplish much." ~ *Blaise Pascal*

The Weight and Wind of our Words

I like to talk. I'm a Chatty Cathy all the way. But the more I talk, the larger chance I have of screwing up my words. Over the years, I have learned (with the help of my husband) that it's better to trim back the amount of verbiage I spew and to intentionally pick and choose - to control this little tongue of mine.

Even commonplace and seemingly trivial words carry *much* weight to them. Proverbs 18:21 tells us, in fact, that "*the tongue has the power of life and death.*"

Whoa. Really? Should we be taking our vocabulary that seriously? Well, let's stop and think about it. Have you ever had your day completely made by something someone said to you? I sure have. A simple compliment or encouragement can leave you flying high as it breathes life into your day. On the other hand, a miniscule passing criticism can cut you to the core and completely derail your day. We certainly should not live by the praises of others but the world is absolutely a better place when we lift one another up with our words, rather than pummeling each other with them.

Our words are also telling. They often disclose what we are thinking. In her life elevating book, *Commanding Your Morning,* Dr. Cindy Trimm teaches us, *"Words reveal what's going on in your heart: "Whatever you harbor in the innermost corridors of your thought life will, sooner or later, reveal itself in the outer arena through your words or actions."*[9] So, what do your words say about you? In what direction do *your* words move you and others?

It doesn't take much imagination to compare our words to the wind. You can't see them but you sure can feel them and spot their effects everywhere. Their invisible power is mighty enough to completely redirect the current of a conversation. They can be weighty enough to defeat deception or wild enough to devastate dear friends. They can be frigid enough to take all the heat out of the room or warm enough to breathe new life into it. Which way do the winds of your words blow? Are they weathered by the Word of God or free to wander on their own?

Church Chatter

Ladies of the church, our words don't always sound like they should. In fact, a lot of the time we sound no different than our friends who don't yet have Christ to help them. You may be familiar with the "Housewives" reality TV series (if not, it is one of the worst examples of how women should treat one another). Dare I say, sometimes our church chatter sounds an awful lot like "The Housewives of Bethel, Glad Tidings or First Assembly." It is the sad truth that we can be just as catty, critical, judgmental and untruthful as the rest of them. Perhaps we know how to wrap our harsh words up in a prettier, more spiritual sounding bow or couch our criticisms in softer language, but the content is still the same. So, let us not forget this:

> *"Don't speak evil against each other dear brothers and sisters. If you criticize and judge each other, then you are criticizing and judging God's law."*
> ~ *James 4:11*

We call each other "sisters" and yet we toss around gossip masked as "prayer requests" and throw stones with our mouths under the guise of "standing up for righteousness". God sees through our attempts at making holy what is not holy and He *will* hold us accountable.

Don't "Be Little"

The things you say about others speak volumes about you. Now, some of us don't mean to be mean. It may have been modeled for us or directed towards us, which left us feeling small. You see, those who can't bring themselves to compliment another woman, or who belittle them, often do so because they have been made to feel little themselves. Whether words have been spoken well of us or not, it is a battle within all of us to choose a higher road with the words we speak of others.

In many cases, those who cut others down with their

words are ones who are not confident in themselves. But, the truth is you will never feel bigger by belittling someone else. Stepping on other women will never make you taller. And, trying to make another woman look bad will *never* make you look good. I promise, though, when you speak well of the women around you, others will see the best in you.

If you find that a woman is doing her best to take you down a notch with her words, remember this - no one can make you feel inferior without your consent. And, most of the time *she* is the one who is feeling inferior, so do your best to extend her some grace and some kind words of your own.

Gossip Girl, Be Gone!

Gossip Girl was a popular and glamorous television show based in the Upper East side of New York City. The star, Blake Lively, is as cute as a button. But gossip isn't cute, nor is it classy. Gossip is ugly.

Don't be led to believe that it is any good at all. While the world finds gossip harmless and enjoyable, God knows that gossip causes grief, so He warns us of the damage done by loose lips.

> *"A troublemaker plants seeds of strife; gossip separates the best of friends." ~ Proverbs 16:28 (NLT)*

> *"A gossip betrays a confidence, but a trustworthy person keeps a secret." ~ Proverbs 11:13 (NIV)*

One of the fastest ways we can damage relationship is

by allowing or spreading gossip. We must all evaluate our conversations and make certain we are not leaking information that is not ours to divulge. We must also be careful to praise others behind their backs, rather than speaking poorly of them.

Do you ever wonder what another woman must say about you outside of your company when she is ripping shreds off, or giving nitty gritty details about another woman to you? I definitely do. Remember, if she gossips *to* you, she will gossip *about* you. What Susie says of Sally says *more* about *Susie* than Sally. It says that Susie is not trustworthy. Think about this:

> *"When you tell someone something that you're suppose to be keeping a secret, and you ask him/her to promise not to tell anyone, what you're doing is hoping that he is more honorable and trustworthy than you are!"* ~ R.Morris

Don't be someone who makes others wonder if you are speaking negatively about them. And, when someone begins to share secrets that are not meant for you, make sure they stop at your ears. Better yet, put a halt to them *before* they enter your ears! Gossip dies when it enters the ears of the wise.

Believe a Fraction of What You Hear and Only Half of What You See

Years ago a young girl made a not-so-wise move that cost a former pastor of ours much grief. Our pastor was still in Seminary at the time and was sifting through some items in the trunk of his car. He needed both hands for this job so he stuck the white Bic pen he had been holding into his mouth. Unbeknownst to him, a girl spotted him from across the parking lot and from her vantage point, concluded our pastor (then student) was smoking a cigarette on school grounds - something strictly prohibited at this Seminary. Of course, this righteous young woman felt it her duty to report him to the Dean's office. After all, an act like this one should never go unpunished! A short time later, our pastor found himself in the Dean's office having to explain himself, and why he "stooped so low" as to smoke a...*Bic pen.*

You see, ladies - even our very own eyes can deceive us, so we must never assume that what our ears hear is gospel truth. Not even what you see may be the truth. Remember this story when you are tempted to share news that isn't yours to share. And even when the news *is* ours to share, most of the time it isn't necessary or helpful to do so.

Stirring the Pot Makes Your Heart Rot

I know I'm not the only woman who loves to chit chat. Women connect by communicating with one another. The problem is that too often we connect by communicating *about* other women.

"Did you see what she was wearing on the platform last Sunday?" Gasp. *"That could tempt our teen boys."*

"Can you believe how her husband has been treating her? I feel so badly."

"What's with her kids getting away with that kind of behavior? Someone should say something."

Do you see how simple it can be to disguise words we are never meant to discuss as concern and care? All this type of conversation accomplishes is making situations more unsettled - it just *stirs the pot*. All too often we discuss with others what we should be discussing with The Lord. Even your best friend doesn't need to know every juicy detail about the other women in your lives.

I have a friend who has reason to share a similar negative opinion as me about someone. It is tempting to talk, but all that would do is stir the pot and make our hearts rot. I'll admit, it is usually her restraint that has kept me in check. I am so glad. I know that nothing good will ever come from godless chatter. It not only hurts others, it fuels negative thoughts and allows junk to fester in us. The result is almost always dissension, anger and strife between others and within ourselves. So, remember that *"Too much talk leads to sin. Be sensible and keep your mouth shut!"* - Proverbs 10:19

Zip Your Lip

Solomon was spot on when he warned us to keep our mouths shut. He said even a fool who keeps silent is considered wise (Proverbs 17:28). I am learning the value of his instruction more and more. Sometimes more can be fixed with tight lips than hours of conversation.

James 3:6 likens our tongue to a fire. Even though it's small, it's as dangerous as a tiny spark that can set a whole forest ablaze. But, as my mother-in-law says, *"Where there is no wood, the fire goes out"*. So, taste your words before you spit them out to make sure they will not burn others.

Keep your negative thoughts about other women to yourself, ladies! Do whatever you can to squash them. When we share them, we can dramatically influence others' opinions with even one piddly remark. Whether your views are misjudged or quite accurate, let others form their own opinions. As we learn to use discretion with our words, and when we shouldn't speak at all, our relationships are rescued from strain and even disaster. Proverbs 13:13 says "He who guards his mouth preserves his life". This also goes for the life of our friendships.

The Circle of Life

We understand now that the words we speak can negatively impact other women and our relationships with them, but they can also give life!

We can use our words to heal broken hearts and relationships. We can facilitate inclusion where there has been division. We can plant seeds of confidence. We can use our words like water to refresh others. The great news is that Proverbs 11:25 says *"Those who refresh others will themselves be refreshed."* The benefits aren't just for others. They are for you too! When you speak well of others, you save yourself a wealth of problems and avoid sticky situations. You will gain trust and respect as others speak highly of you. Your conscience will be clear, and that's a great feeling. You will bless others, and that's a really great feeling. You will be the kind of gal that everyone wants to be around!

Think Things Through

We all want to be someone others want to be around, but it can certainly be a challenge to use discretion with our words. Here is a handy acrostic I heard years ago on our local Christian radio station that has kept me in check.

THINK before you speak:
Check to make sure what you're about to say is:

T rue
H elpful
I nspiring
N ecessary
K ind

"Let the words of my mouth and the mediation of my heart be acceptable in your sight, oh God, my strength and redeemer." ~ Psalm 19:14

I Wish I Had Known...

...To address hurtful words right away and the *right* way.

"My closest friends and I were on a girl's trip recently and one of the topics that came up was the power of our words. Ironically, the last night of our trip, we'd had a long day and everyone was tired, irritable and things got a little tense. We said some things and used some tones that we shouldn't have. When we got in the car to go out to dinner, the atmosphere was still strained. One friend finally said, "OK, ladies, let's talk about this. If anyone was hurt or offended by words that were spoken, let's just deal with it head-on and make sure everything is ok. It's ok to not be ok, but it's not ok to not talk about it!"

Her words opened the door for each of us to share how we felt about what took place, instead of stewing about it all night and pretending things were fine. We made a commitment that night to address any conflict, whenever it arises, as soon as we can, even if it's awkward or uncomfortable. I wish I would have adopted this principle years ago - it would have saved me many lost hours of sleep!"

~ "Ella"

 ## Reflective Questions

~ How would I feel knowing other women were belittling, gossiping or "stirring the pot" about me?

~ How can I use my words to give life to another woman this week, or even today?!

CHAPTER 14
Blend in Blessing

*"It won't mean you're weak if you turn the
other cheek" ~ Kenny Rogers*

It's Nice to be Nice...to the Nice

Frank Burns (M.A.S.H.) said it best: *"It's nice to be nice...
to the nice."*

Isn't it though? When I'm given a compliment, it obviously strokes my ego. When someone lets me cut in line, my mood brightens. When a co-worker agrees with me, I feel validated. In all these cases I can effortlessly return the gesture. When everything is nicey-nice, it's *easy* to be nice.

But, what about when the Volvo takes a sharp turn out of nicey-nice-ville? How should we respond to the ones whose opinions differ from ours, who's attitudes towards us are less than lovely, or who seem like they're plain out to get us?

If we're convinced God's ways are best, we should take careful consideration of the counsel Paul gives us in Romans 12:14-16:
"Bless those who persecute you. Don't curse them;

*pray that God will bless them…live in harmony
with each other."*

I can hear you all saying "Yeah right! You're kidding me!" Paul wasn't out to get a laugh here. He was teaching the very words of Christ:

*"You have heard that it has been said "an eye for an
eye and a tooth for a tooth". But I say to you, do not
resist evil; but whosoever shall strike you on your
right cheek, turn to him the other also…You have
heard that it has been said, "You shall love your
neighbor and hate your enemy." But I say to you:
Love your enemies, bless those who curse you, do
good to those who hate you, and pray for those who
mistreat you, and persecute you."*
~ Matthew 5:38, 43, 44

It's Nicer to be Nice to the Nasty

Jesus' methods are counter-cultural and often opposite of what *feels* right. Who of us feels like loving someone unlovable? He is clear though, that we are to love our enemies. I know, I know. That's not my first inclination either. We must *choose* love. We must choose to bless. This is no small feat. We will grapple daily with love choices and need the Holy Spirit to help us. But, when we are able to love our enemies, that's when things start getting real. That is when the world will see Christ's love in a tangible way. Anyone can love a friend, but when we bless those who persecute us, we rock their world, as we unveil a God who does the impossible.

Turning the Other Cheek

Author of *True Spirituality*, Chip Ingram, shares a story with his readers that helped me make sense of what Jesus was saying in Matthew 5. It involves a man who persecuted him throughout his college years. Jimmy, a reformed drug addict, had developed a hard exterior, to say the least, while serving in the armed forces. Evil dug its claws into Jimmy's life and caused him to become evil towards others. Chip, his college basketball teammate, was one of his regular victims. Jimmy harassed, publicly humiliated, ridiculed and even threatened Chip's life. Chip candidly describes his inward battle of wanting to get Jimmy back for what he did to him. He wanted revenge and he fantasized how to get it. He admitted he didn't just want to curse Jimmy - he wanted to kill him. He confided in a ministry leader who surprised him with the challenge to kill Jimmy with kindness instead. It woke up Chip's willingness to do what Christ tells us and bless the one who was persecuting him (Romans 12:14-21).

Chip accepted his confidant's challenge and, from that point on, considered himself Jimmy's friend and even his servant. He no longer wished for revenge opportunities but he responded to Jimmy's evil with good.

"For the next four months Jimmy never had to ask. 'Hey Jimmy, I've got your bag; I put it in the bus. Anything else I can get for you?'... 'Jimmy, I'm going back for seconds (at the team meal), can I get you a Coke or another piece of meat?'...When Jimmy went to the shower, I gathered his sweaty practice gear, put it in the nylon bag, gave it to the trainer to be

> *washed, and then folded his clothes*
> *next to his locker."*[10]

This, ladies, is turning the other cheek.

Well, what happened with Chip and Jimmy? Initially, Jimmy's rage heightened. He asked Chip if this was some sort of "Christian trick" he was playing on him. Eventually Jimmy's harassment subsided and his heart somewhat softened towards Chip. Chip noticed that as he served Jimmy, his heart had softened too. He was no longer plagued with hatred but was compelled towards compassion for this man who he once detested. At the end of the basketball season, Jimmy admitted to Chip:

> *"There are only two people on this team that I*
> *respect: me, 'cause I'm evil and I know it and I'm*
> *on my way to hell if there is one..and you. I disagree*
> *with every single thing you say and believe, but if I*
> *was even in any way going to become a Christian,*
> *I'd have to say that I'd want to be one like you... I'm*
> *done messin' with your mind, kid.*
> *I'll leave you alone."*

Jimmy didn't fall to his knees in repentance at that moment but he now had experienced Christ's love through Chip. Chip had done his job.

Whether or not the woman who is mistreating you will beg forgiveness from you, it is our mandate to turn the other cheek and show them Christ's love. It makes a whole lot of sense, and this is why:

"Loving our enemies - feeding them when they're hungry and giving them a drink when they are thirsty - is the most powerful apologetic on the face of the earth. Loving people who don't deserve to be loved in a way they don't deserve or expect can break through the hardest hearts and demonstrate the reality of the living God like few other things in the entire world." ~ Chip Ingram

I firmly believe that when we do our best, God does the rest. We simply need to live in full surrender to Him and His methods. So, is surrender a sign of weakness? When we give in to God and our enemies, does that mean we are weaklings? Chip's story proved to me that we can truly impact others, and our own lives for good, when we turn the other cheek...

Pansies and Pushovers?

Was Chip being a pansy or a pushover? Absolutely not! In fact, he displayed backbone that many of us do not normally see. Self-preservation doesn't require the strength that turning the other cheek does. God isn't wimpy either. He is mighty to save and He will respond to any wrong done to you.

Having said that, things will go well for us when we handle ourselves in a Christ-like way. God is smart and His ways work. Blessing others and choosing to love the ones who persecute us doesn't equal getting trampled on. Chip offered Jimmy grace and love. It was on his own terms. He didn't barrel him down in anger, neither did he cower in a corner. He was gentle and humbled himself towards his enemy. And, you can do the same. Being meek doesn't mean you are weak.

An Eye for an Eye Doesn't Fly

What has become clear to me all the more while studying for this chapter is that "an eye for an eye" never gets us anywhere other than in an even bigger heap of trouble than we started with. We think we'll feel better if we give her "what's coming to her", but we won't. Revenge never satisfies because it leaves everything unsettled. Revenge doesn't cure feelings of anger, anxiousness or pain but often heightens them. So, trust God enough to step away and let *Him* deal with her, even though every fibre of your being wants to take matters into your own hands.

Curtains, Walls and the Cold War

Maybe you're thinking: "Danielle, I'm Miss *Un*confrontational. I wouldn't hurt a fly. I'm way too chicken to take matters into my own hands or even give that girl a piece of my mind. I just stay far *far* away." Does that mean your *heart* does not have enemies? If you have contempt for someone, even if it's buried down deep, the following paragraphs are for you.

At first glance, perhaps you thought this book may not be for you, after all, you "get along" with others. You don't have someone ridiculing you regularly, like Chip, nor have you experienced the drama of a Housewives of Orange County type "chick fight", complete with hair pulling and spilled martinis.

We are much more put together on the outside. There are no torn blouses or bloody fingernails, but if we take a peek at what lies beneath, we may find a bloody mess. Pumping through the crevices of your heart, unable to be detected with the naked eye, there could be a ticking time bomb of indignation, contempt, spite, or any of the spoilers found in the beginning pages of this book. There may very well be a *Cold War* going on beneath the surface of your Christian niceties. And, it may just be killing you.

By no means am I a history buff, but I certainly have heard of The Iron Curtain. Not made of any palpable substance, The Iron Curtain was a symbol of the divide in Europe from the end of World War 2 to the end of The Cold War. An actual concrete boundary was constructed in Germany, which we knew as the Berlin Wall. This wall was *highly guarded* and *divided* many people for decades.

Pause and ask yourself what barricades you have constructed between you and another woman. Are you too guarded? Have you shut her out? Are there walls that need to be toppled in order for you to be at peace? Is there a Cold War bubbling beneath that begs for resolution?

There is fantastic news for you. The Peacemaker, Jesus, has made a way for you! He has already torn the curtain and provided a way for us to come to Him for help. There are no walls between us and Him, and there doesn't have to be between you and her. He can help topple the walls and bash the bricks between us. He has the ability to soften hearts and turn our Cold Wars into relationships filled with warmth and love.

Doing Good Does a lot of Good

One of the best ways I can think to thaw your cold heart towards another woman is to pray for her. God doesn't tell us to ignore or avoid our enemies like the plague. No, He says to *bless* those who persecute us (or, who simply drive us crazy). It's hard to hate someone you're praying for. He further instructs us to go and do good to them (Matthew 5:44). This seems like an impossibility but, with the help of the Holy Spirit, we are able!

When she mistreats you, pray for her so she can experience the same grace you have also been given. This is a powerful, unifying act. I know it can be a challenge but praise specific things about her... remind others of her strengths and say kind things to her and about her. Puff HER up! Furthermore, GO and DO something good for her. You may have to force it initially, but act kindly towards her. Do the things you know are right and eventually it won't be an act any more.

"Bless those who persecute you. Don't curse them; pray that God will bless them...live in harmony with each other." ~ Romans 12:14-16

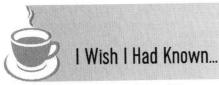

I Wish I Had Known...

... That my reputation lives longer than my anger.

"I was never severely bullied during my school years, but there were definitely a few girls who picked on me. Most of the time I handled it well, but occasionally I didn't.

When I was thirteen, I certainly wasn't thinking about who I'd be when I was thirty. And, I definitely wouldn't have imagined that with today's technology, I'd still be connected to some of these girls, becoming "friends" on social media. Some of the girls who *picked on me* now *look to me* as a leader.

If I had realized that when I was young, I'm certain I would have handled myself towards them much better. My frustration with them for mocking me because I lived differently, would have been less severe if I had known they would one day look to me for prayers and advice. This knowledge will continue to motivate me towards love whenever I feel misunderstood, belittled or persecuted.

So, young ladies, remember this: if handled with care, the one who harasses you today may turn into one who honors you tomorrow."

~ Danielle Macaulay

Reflective Questions

~ Who has loved me when I have been unlovable?

~ Who needs *me* to overlook offence, and turn the other cheek in mercy?

~ What good can I practically do for someone who has mistreated me?

~ How might this impact our relationship?

CHAPTER 15
A Gram of Gratitude

"The struggle ends when gratitude begins."
~ Neale Donald Walsch

The "Woe is Me" Disability

Much like the comparison trap, most of us at some point fall into the pit of ungratefulness. A *"woe is me"* epidemic is growing exponentially, especially in North America. Just flick the channel on to HGTV's "House Hunters" for five minutes and you'll find women who are reduced to toddler behavior because their potential new home might not have double sinks! It is all too easy to look around at what others have and think we are hard done by. I have discovered the remedy to this disease is shifting our perspective by taking our eyes off of others and putting them on the Lord. We must also develop a chronic case of thankfulness because an unthankful heart is the breeding ground for so much that plagues our relationships and causes strife amongst us. When we look at another woman and count *her* blessings instead of our own, we look at her with envy and contempt. Beware when your heart hardens towards her and towards God because a hardened heart is the most serious of all conditions.

We Need a Remedy to our Malady

The good news is that God has provided an antidote. First, we must be willing to admit we have fallen victim and are part of this pesky pandemic. Do you feel grumpy and debilitated from too many walks down the path of envy? Have you unwarrantedly whined, like a toddler who pouts over receiving the green cup instead of the pink one? Has your heart become calloused from the friction that coveting her life causes? Do you blame God for your "misfortune"? Have you not given Him enough credit for the surplus of blessings that have been poured into your cup?

God has designed us with great purpose and gifted us with blessing beyond what we deserve. He does immeasurably more than we could ask or imagine, yet often we choose to set our eyes on what we think we're missing. Why on Earth do we focus on our deficiencies so much?

Without doubt, it has to do with what we feed our minds. We perpetually ingest the idea fed to us that we need more. Yet, this imperfect life doesn't deliver the ideals for which this world says we need to work tirelessly. Keeping up with the Jones' is a full-time job with no benefits. When we keep our eyes on what we lack rather than what we possess, and strive for what is out of reach, we will suffer the consequences. There will always be a nagging misery and disappointment we won't be able to shake.

If you feel exhausted from living ungratefully and ready to move on to better things, let me tell you the remedy: *Gratitude* melts our begrudgingly ungrateful, ailing hearts.

How to Generate and Grow Gratitude

Media constantly bombards us with reasons why we need just a *bit* more than we have now. It guilts us and grips us into believing we should have better than we do. It taunts us with lies that there are women around us who are living the life we dream of. This sways us into attitudes of *in*gratitude.

Ungrateful attitudes will leak toxic waste all over our relationships. It is very hard to feel and be loving towards someone you've allowed to be the object of your envy and disdain. You will always feel inferior and angry around them.

There have been times I nosedived right into the pit of ungratefulness. The law of gravity seems to be ever more founded when we're falling hard. Here are a few ways that helped me heft my way out and make certain that gratitude kept me on solid ground with God *and* with my girlfriends.

1. Count Your Blessings - Not Hers

The old hymn tells us, "Count *your* blessings, name them one by one." (Johnson Oatman Jr.). It doesn't say to count *hers*. When we keep a closer eye on another woman's blessings instead of ours, it will blind us to the goodness God has graced us with. Be certain that ingratitude will rear its ugly head. While it is true there are women surrounding us with abilities, relationships and material possessions we long for, it is important to realize another woman may be praying for your blessings.

Yes, you're right - you will not look like, talk like, sing like, run like, have a home like, have a job like, have a ministry like, have a purse like, have those legs like or have a husband like her. But, there is a woman out there - maybe closer than you think - who is adding up all *your* blessings you have neglected to calculate. Our blessings come in different packages but we all have them. You'll find more when you start looking for them.

Ann Voskamp discovered the vast benefits of counting her blessings and writes about it in her bestselling book *One Thousand Gifts*. She documents a thousand ways, big and small, she has been given good things by God. She finds that gratitude for even the smallest thing creates substantial abundance in her life. She says:

> *"The miracle of multiplying happens when I give thanks."*[11]

Author Melodie Beattie agrees with Ann:

> *"Gratitude unlocks the fullness of life. It turns what we have into enough, and more...It can turn a meal into a feast, a house into a home, a stranger into a friend. Gratitude makes sense of our past, brings peace for today, and creates a vision for tomorrow."*[12]

When we give thanks intentionally and regularly, an ungrateful heart will give way to the overflow of bountiful blessing. God's goodness will break the dam that divides us between others and Himself. So, take Ann's lead and begin to jot down, journal or simply say thank you more than you ever have. Look for the beauty in the everyday and stay conscious of your blessings. This will absolutely shift your perspective...from lack to abundance!

2. Change your perspective

We must remember that our vantage point is skewed. We don't fully see the whole picture. Our view of God is like that of someone peering through beveled or stained glass. There are moments of clarity but, for the most part, our vision is impaired as we gaze through a distorted, foggy lens. The external influencers in media that I mentioned earlier, muddy the picture even more. The neat thing about this type of glass though, is that if we shift ourselves and look through a different location, we may see better than we did before.

We're in need of a perspective shift, ladies. We need to pick ourselves up and allow our minds to move in the right direction. How we do this is with the Word of God. Psalm 119:105 tells us that God's Word is a lamp unto our feet, and a light unto our path. It helps us see the best way to go and think correct thoughts. It offers clarity to the broken, stained, ideas that the enemy leads us to believe.

In *One Thousand Gifts*, Ann Voskamp teaches us, "*Without God's Word as a lens, the world warps.*"[13] God's word is truly what will help us refocus. It is the lens we should put on to view our entire lives.

Here are a few exercises that will help you re-focus on God's Word:

◆   Write down the things you feel ungrateful about. Replace those thoughts with what God says about the matter. Then go through and cross out the thoughts that are not true. You will find that your story becomes pretty thin and God's truth will hold.

◆   Meditate on that truth and ask God to help you see things differently. God has the power to change your mind. Pray and ask God to fill your mind with how *He* sees your circumstances. Your life moves in the direction of your strongest thoughts (Craig Groeschel). When we fill our minds with God-given thoughts, we will move towards higher and greater things.

◆   Give yourself *time*. Everything seems worse in the moment. Time is a great perspective shifter. As mentioned in another chapter, our feelings are flighty - and often fictional, so give time for the dust to settle.

3. Take Your Eyes Off Of Her and Put Them On Him

It is truly remarkable how quickly the good things in our lives become overshadowed by the attention we place on other women's lives. Comparison really does steal our joy - by making us ungrateful. The blessing of a new vehicle we've been needing for some time seems wonderful to us - that is until we see a Ray Ban clad woman whiz by us in her brand new BMW. We may be feeling quite content with the decor in our homes...until we tune in to the newest episode of Fixer Upper and decide that Joanna Gaines puts us to shame. We are impressed with our children's grades in school, until the neighbor gushes about her kids making the honor roll. And, we will always feel like we've got a hard knock life when we flip through the pages of a magazine filled with the lifestyles of the rich and the famous.

Suddenly, we aren't enough, we don't have enough and God isn't enough. Comparisons will keep us discontented and deflated, perpetuating an ungrateful heart.

Here are some suggestions on how to take your eyes off of her and put them on God.

- Take a break from Social Media and get face to face with women who will remind you of all your blessings.
- Trash your trashy magazines and open your Bible.
- Turn off the tube and read *One Thousand Gifts* by Ann Voskamp.

Social Media, home decor, fashion, beauty and gossip magazines, and the television are the top offenders for giving us material that will instantly make us miserable. If we eliminate, or at least reduce, these influencers and replace them with better things, it will help us focus on the beauty that surrounds us and all God has given us.

Life Isn't Always Rosy - But Your attitude Makes it Rosier

Maybe your life is not overly rosy right now. It can be difficult to recognize God's goodness in difficult seasons. But, we are instructed to give thanks in *every* circumstance (1 Thess. 5:18). If you are feeling like you got the "green cup", and not the pink one, rejoice that you have a vessel to drink in the blessing! Stop dwelling on the fact that your cup is not as rosy. God loves to give good gifts to his children and, I promise you, there is sustenance in that cup, no matter the color. Give thanks in the midst of the suffering. Take Paul's lead and look for the good, whatever you may be faced with. You will not be put to shame.

> *"Not only that, but we rejoice in our sufferings, knowing that suffering produces endurance, and endurance produces character, and character produces hope, and hope does not put us to shame, because God's love has been poured into our hearts through the Holy Spirit who has been given to us."*
> *~ Romans 5:3-5*

From "Woe" To "Wow"

When we actively look for the good in ourselves, others and God, things begin to change.

You may have been used to closing your hands to shake a fist at God. When you do this, you prevent Him from filling it with anything. But, when you focus on what you have been given; what is in your hands, you open yourself up to receive more blessing. Your hands are open and ready to be filled even more - and there is option for overflow. *Gratitude allows our hands to be lifted up and cupped together as a bowl, creating a vessel for God to fill.* Gratitude also provides joy, peace and a life filled with awe at the wonders God has granted you with. Here are two men who completely prove my point:

"Sherlock Holmes and Dr. Watson are camping.

They pitch their tent under the stars and go to sleep.
Sometime in the middle of the night, Holmes wakes
Watson up. Holmes: "Watson, look up at the stars,
and tell me what you deduce." Watson: "I see mil-
lions of stars and even if a few of those have planets,
it's quite likely there are some planets like earth, and
if there are a few planets like earth out there, there
might also be life. What does it tell you, Holmes?"
Holmes: "Watson, you idiot, somebody has stolen
our tent!"[14] (Geoff Anandappa)

So, will you choose to focus on what you don't have, or what's been *taken* from you? Or will you choose to see what has been *given* to you? Sherlock or Watson; who had the better view?

"Give thanks to the Lord, for he is good. His love
endures forever" ~ Psalm 107:1

I Wish I Had Known...

...To unwrap my own gifts.

"One would think that after growing up with four sisters, I might know all there is to know when navigating through the ups and downs that can come in women's friendships. I realize now that, whether you have many sisters or no sisters, there are a few things I wish I had understood about myself and the women I'd meet throughout life.

When I was young and still living at home with my parents and four other sisters, the differences in the personality and talents among the five girls was beautiful and God ordained. However, we didn't always look at it that way! My younger sister was an incredible athlete and excelled in competitive gymnastics. She was so talented that my parents enrolled her in a gymnastics school an hour and a half from our home and regularly drove her to practice five nights a week.

Instead of finding something that I was gifted in, I tried to be a great gymnast just like my sister.

Many years later, while on a women's retreat, I thought about this again. I saw a picture in my mind of a large basket of beautifully wrapped gifts. I saw the Lord take the basket of gifts and hand them out to everyone. Each woman started to unwrap her beautiful gift but, as she did, she began to look at the other women's gifts and turn her attention from the very gift that had been given to her.

It was then the Lord showed me that each of us has been given one or more incredible gifts from Him. Instead of admiring it and using it, however, we compare what we have with what another has. This very act causes us to want to be like someone else because we see how wonderful another woman's gift is. The more we focus on this comparison, the more the door opens to jealousy and envy. We experience jealousy instead of joy, misery instead of ministry.

Where is the beautifully wrapped gift you've been given? Is it still unwrapped collecting dust in the closet of insecurity because you don't think it is as beautiful as someone else's? What friendships in your life have stopped growing because of this comparison with one another? Proverbs 18:16 says that "a man's gift makes room for him and brings him before great men." Open up your gift and God will make room for you!"

~ Terri Kelly

Reflective Questions

~ What other woman's blessings have I been counting too much?

~ When it comes to looking at the good in my own life, am I Watson or Holmes?

CHAPTER 16
A Quart of Confidence

"Everyone is a genius. But if you judge a fish on its ability to climb a tree, it will live its whole life believing that it's stupid" ~ Albert Einstein

"Always be a first-rate version of yourself, instead of a second-rate version of somebody else".
~ Judy Garland

Feelings and "Fake News"

When we feel we've been robbed, we'll want to steal from others. When we don't know our worth, or the vast treasure that we are, we'll try to snatch it from someone else. But, feelings aren't what we go on, right gals?

Ann Voskamp tells the truth in *The Broken Way*:

> *"Feelings are meant to be felt and given to God - but feelings can't tell you about God, you or your relationship. Your identity, your security, your acceptability come from who God is - and not how you feel. Because, there was something before what you felt about yourself - and that is what God feels about you."*[21]

Feelings are flighty and often fictional. Depending on what you ate, how much you (*didn't*) sleep or who you've been hanging around, like an uninformed weatherman, your feelings will fail you. Maybe someone said that you didn't mean anything to them. Perhaps you believed a lie that said nobody cares. Surely you've felt ugly and stupid before. Let me tell you; you are loved, wanted...desired. You are *needed* in this world. Don't believe the "fake news" about you.

Stop trying to attain what others have and begin to focus on discovering what *you* have to offer. In order to do this, you must first take your eyes off others and resist the comparison game. I hope my chapter on Comparison has helped you do just that. Now, I must steer you in the right direction; towards the One who knows you more intimately than your own mother, sister or spouse. Like the manufacturer of a watch knows exactly how and why it ticks, as your maker, God knows you intricately - exactly how *you* tick. He's the only one who holds the right to define you. What does God have to say about you?

First of all, your Heavenly Father, your creator, loves *you* uniquely. In *Without Rival*, Lisa Bevere effectively convinces her reader (thankfully, one of those readers was me) that God made her and loves her so uniquely, and that it's more than just a Christian feel good cliche. She says,

"*He authored how your heart expresses itself; He was the architect of your smile and the melody of your voice; He made all of your features with the fondest thoughts of only you in mind...He didn't have another daughter in mind when He fashioned you.... you are His delight. This means you wouldn't do it better if you*

were taller, shorter, more black or white...there is absolutely noth-
ing accidental about you...You don't have to fight for your place at
the table or win His love. No one can take you out or replace you...
you have no rival."[22]

When you dig deep in God's word, you'll discover that you're more than you have given yourself credit for....

The authority of your life and identity (whether you recognize Him as that, or not) says you are made perfectly and wonderfully (Psalm 139), you are holy and without blame (Ephesians 1:4), you have received power (Mark 16:17,18), wisdom (Ephesians 1:17, 18) and all you need (Philippians 4:19). He says you can do all things through Him (Philippians 4:13), that you're more than a conqueror (Romans 8:37) and that you have been chosen by Him (1 Peter 2:9). Did you hear that?! God says that you're a perfect, holy, blameless babe who's powerful, wise and has the ability to conquer. He chose you to be you. He knows that you are more than enough. Have you *felt* like this kind of woman lately? No? Me neither. It's ok - remember that our feelings can lead us astray.

Clones and Counterfeits

There was a girl I thought was pretty, popular, gifted and "had it all" when I was a teen. I remember trying hard to be like her....her talents, mannerisms, style...even her voice. I was trying to clone her but I was just a counterfeit. It just didn't work the same for me as it did for her. She was living authentically and I was just a fraud. For a time, I was not comfortable in my skin or excelling in who God made me because I was too busy focusing on her. I was the stupid fish who was trying to climb the tree and like my friend, Terri, who was trying to be her gymnast sister. It just didn't work, because we are all designed differently.

So, don't try to be someone you're not. You'll never make it. You'll remain perpetually frustrated. God made you just so, to a T, and for very good reason. You'll never excel doing something that you aren't called, built and equipped to do. You'll never be her clone - only a counterfeit. But, you bring God glory when you're authentically you and when you carry out His commission for *your* life. The bonus is that you will look and feel your best as a result. You will shine. People will admire you when they see God in you. That is *really* what you're admiring in the women who are living to their fullest God-given potential. You're admiring the glory of God revealed in them.

Cowering Culprits

The glory of God makes demons flee. Being who God designed you to be will send darkness to the corners. This is one reason I believe Paul exhorted the Romans:

"So since we find ourselves fashioned into all these excellently formed and marvelously functioning parts in Christ's body, let's just go ahead and be what we were made to be, without enviously or pridefully comparing ourselves with each other, or trying to be something we aren't." ~ Romans 12:5,6 (MSG)

Your ability to celebrate what God is doing in someone's

else's life reveals how secure you are in who He is in your life. So, are you secure enough in your identity in Christ to be thankful for what Christ is doing in others? Begin by thanking God for what He's doing in your life right now and who He's made you to be. Do more swimming and less climbing. Spend more time attempting to clone God than the gal you envy on your Instagram feed. Recognize the gifts He's given you and how He is shaping you. Ask the Lord how He wants you to use your distinct gifts to help others and to reveal His glory to them. I assure you that when you live as the best version of you, you will be confident and satisfied, and others will be blessed! Do not rob the world of you!

> *"True confidence is not found in the mirror until it is settled in the soul."* ~ *Catrina Welch*

> *"For you created my inmost being; you knit me together in my mother's womb. I praise you because I am fearfully and wonderfully made; your works are wonderful, I know that full well."*
> ~ *Psalm 139:13, 14*

I Wish I Had Known...

...To look at myself the way that God looks at me - as His daughter!

"When I think back over my growing years, and the relationships with others I had, I wish I would have truly understood how beautiful it is when you understand "whose" you are - understanding that you are royalty and a daughter of the King of Kings. As a teen, I am not sure I really thought about that. So much of what you think about as a teen is acceptance, validation, and affirmation. Unfortunately, as a teen I missed the value of seeing how those 3 things would have come so much easier if I had understood that I was a daughter of the King.

Seeing ourselves "Through His eyes" changes everything. We would see ourselves as loved, covered in grace and mercy, the apple of His eye, His beloved, His cherished one, pure, radiant, and His beautiful daughter that He delights in.

If I had caught the vision of who God says I am, and if I could have seen myself through His eyes, I would have changed how I carried myself in my teen years.

Statistics say that one single characteristic that men (and really, everyone) find extremely attractive in women is confidence. When a woman has confidence in who she is and understands "whose" she is, true and beautiful confidence blossoms. She walks taller, talks stronger, and radiates joy. She is a woman who is not trying to outshine the other woman because she is not in competition. She is thankful for the very moment she is in and understands God made her special and unique. She accepts that He never intended her to be 'like' anyone else and is at ease with herself. She can see her strengths and weaknesses and allow the friendships God sends her to be as 'iron sharpens iron.' She can grow and learn from those who do better than her at various things because she has a humble heart that is focused on Christ and not herself.

I realized during my high school years that, when I just stopped caring what anyone thought about me, and I just started BEING who He called me to be, suddenly people were drawn to me. I stopped defending my faith and began to be proud of my faith. I began to just be what He wanted me to be. This changed everything for me and I wish I would have realized it even younger."

~ Jeanette Willis

 Reflective Questions

- In what ways have I tried to be something I am not; a "counterfeit"?

- Am I able to genuinely celebrate other women's beauty, talents, achievements and blessings?

- Who does God say that I am?

Section 3

CONSEQUENCES
(OF NOT GETTING ALONG)

CHAPTER 17
The Consequences

"Wisdom consists of the anticipation of consequences." ~ Norman Cousins

Residual Repercussions

I hope that this book has inspired and equipped you to become more like Christ in your heart and your daily interactions with the women you're surrounded by. I am certain that when we live according to His ways, our relationships will be blessed and we will be better for it. I would be remiss though, if I did not also disclose the results and realities of *not* "getting along". After all, we are free to choose how to act, but we are not free from the consequences of our actions. Thank God that He forgives us and wipes our slates clean when we repent, but our lives are still a product of the choices we make. There may still be some residual repercussions.

How will our lives be affected when we choose not to live in harmony with one another? What are the ramifications of allowing ourselves to remain bound in our personal issues, which hinder healthy relationships? Here are a few of the major consequences that surely await us when we choose not to get along...

Consequence #1 ~ Isolation

Some of my most cherished, hilarious and impactful moments have been with my girlfriends. Godly women fill a place in my soul that my husband and sons can't fill. I simply cannot unload, seek advice from or giggle with my men the way I do with my gal pals. God understands that we need each other to make it through this harrowing life. He wants us to be woven together so we can support and strengthen one another. Ecclesiastes 4:9-10 says that two are better than one. If one of us falls down, the other is there to pick them up. We are each other's safety net.

On the other hand, Ecclesiastes goes on to tell us that a person standing alone can be attacked and defeated, which is precisely why our enemy wants us to isolate ourselves. He wants us to put walls around ourselves and keep each other at arm's length. And, that, my friends, is exactly where many of us are - behind bars of recluse. This is pure punishment.

You may know the story, *The Count of Monte Cristo*. The main character, Edmund Dante (brilliantly played by Jim Caviezel in the movie) was sentenced to jail for a crime he did not commit. Seven years into solitary confinement, just as he is about to give up hope, he meets Abbe, another inmate. The two become friends and provide sanity and hope for one another. Eventually, Abbe is the reason that Edmund finds freedom. Without his friend, Edmund wouldn't have survived - physically or mentally. In the movie *Castaway*, Tom Hank's character was also isolated for an extended time on a deserted island. You may remember who - or *what* became his best friend during his stay - a volleyball with a face painted in his own blood, that he affectionately named "Wilson". Every man needs to be face to face with a friend, and every woman does too.

Solitary confinement is among the harshest punishments, and yet, our isolation is often our own doing. We remain disconnected because of our own unforgiveness, inability to hold our tongue, insecurity and pride. (And, these days, we settle for "intimacy" through a screen via social media and text, which clearly isn't cutting it). Our own sin does us in and keeps us from connection.

We cannot effectively pray alongside a woman with whom we carry an offense. Others won't confide in us if we are not trustworthy. When we are insecure or jealous, people will walk on eggshells around us or just steer clear. We become a love repellent when we actually need love the most. Let me remind you of the lady who so bravely confessed to us that she felt like nearly every other woman within sight was better than her, and it caused her to shut the door and stay at home.

On the flip side, ladies, as I mentioned earlier, it can be lonely on top. Pride divides. I look back to my younger years when it felt good to be "on top". There were times my pride got the better of me as it told me I was prettier, smarter, more athletic and talented. All that mentality surely did was isolate me from girls who I made feel inferior. It didn't benefit me at all.

You see how these "spoilers" really do spoil us? Like the opposing ends of a magnet, we cannot connect when we push each other away. If we hide in our houses, or stand high on our pedestals, we will never be within reach when we need someone. We will miss out on party invites, inspiring conversations, and life giving words. We'll definitely not be close enough to have the rough edges smoothed away. We will miss the opportunity to bless others. It will be all about us, leaving no room for others; a selfish place to be.

This is exactly where the enemy wants us. He wants us lonesome and inaccessible, unable to comfort, care for and challenge one another. Our enemy wants our relationships to wither, and there is no faster way for that to happen than when we allow the spoilers to segregate us.

> *"Whoever isolates (herself) seeks (her) own desires;*
> *(she) breaks out against all sound judgement."*
> *~ Proverbs 18:1*

Consequence #2 - Disobedience

As if isolation is depressing enough, it doesn't get any better here, ladies (don't shoot the messenger)! When we are living in disobedience, *especially* when we know better, this does not make our Heavenly Father happy. In 1 Peter 5:5, it says that God "opposes the proud". Yikes! I don't know about you, but I do not want God to oppose me! More than just pride, all of the spoilers are detrimental to our relationships. They are sinful behavior, commonplace as they are. God opposes anything that spoils our hearts because we're called to live in peace (Col 3:13-15). This is a command - not a suggestion.

God takes it personally how we treat one another since we are his daughters. In the same way that children resemble their parents, we resemble Him. So, when He looks at each of us, He sees Himself. I have two kids - sweetest little boys on planet earth in all their noisy, stinky, dirty glory. If you mess with *them*, you mess with *me*. If you aren't treating them right, I'm going to have something to say (or do) about it. Similarly, If we aren't "getting along" with the women around us, God has strong feelings about that. You mess with His little girl, you mess with Him. If you backstab, gossip, speak hurtful, damaging words or hold a grudge against another woman, you've done that against God. If you are destroying *yourself* in any way, He wants to swoop in and put it to a halt as well. He always has something to say about it!

Whether at war with each other or within ourselves, where there is war, there is rebellion. Sadly, rebellion is all too familiar and can feel like home to us. Sin can be cozy. Even those snug insecurity blankets we keep wrapped around ourselves are sinful. It is insatiably attractive to us, but in the end it leads to death.

Since God wants the absolute best (abundant life) for us, He will correct us. Proverbs 3:12 says "The Lord disciplines those he loves, as a father the (daughter) he delights in." He wants to prevent us from further harm and He will go to great lengths to protect His children if they are being attacked.

Consequence #3 - Missing out on God's Blessing

I was married at the not so ripe age of 20 years old. All at once, my marital status changed, I moved to a new country, landed a new job and became a pastor's wife (I believe that's several of life's biggest stressors simultaneously). Looking back, this was crazy! Barely out of my teen years, I was plucked out of the bubble I had grown up in and thrown into a whole new world. This wasn't just any world - Greenwich, Connecticut (home of the rich and famous) felt like a different planet. I was nowhere near prepared for this. I could have used an older, godly woman to help me navigate this marriage, moving and ministerial frontier. I needed support, encouragement and a mentor. I needed a friend and spiritual big sister.

And, she was right in front of me, girls...*literally* sitting across from me at a table in an Italian pub, munching on a gorgonzola salad, offering this very thing to me. *"If there's ever anything you need, I'm here for you. We're here to support you and Dan. We love you guys"*, she assured me. She wanted to be my safety net. She treated me to lunch to tell me this very thing.

The absurd and unfortunate thing is that, although I nodded my head in thanks that day, I didn't take her up on the offer. I foolishly refused the support. I rejected her, even though I wanted and completely needed her. Why on earth would I do that? Well, I told you the story earlier in this book. My own stupid sin got in the way and, when I needed it most, I missed out.

I was so insecure of my shortcomings that I feared getting close to her would magnify my weakness. I deduced that because she had wisdom, resources and talents, it meant I was a failure. I habitually played the comparison game and consistently lost. I was envious of all she had and resentful about what I didn't, yet my pride told me I didn't need her. I attended a lonely pity party of one, instead of embracing the benefits of sisterhood.

As a result, I missed out on many many good things for *way* too long. I missed out on laughs, love, prayers, wise counsel and so much more. Oh, to think who I could have become so much earlier on in life because this godly woman was willing to invest in me. I see clearly now that if I had have continued on in my sin, how much blessing I truly would have missed.

A miracle occured as I unpacked my baggage and repented of my sin. I began to experience the blessing that happens when we walk in obedience. I *now* call this woman friend, confidant and sister... she is single-handedly the most influential woman in my life spiritually. The name that used to send shivers down my spine, the woman who I wanted nothing to do with, is now a name I think of fondly and the woman I look forward to communing with the most. This is because of Jesus and because I chose to smother my sin.

I know what I missed out on, because now I am enjoying the blessing of our friendship. The one I once viewed as my enemy (really, I was my own worst enemy) has been my faithful prayer partner for over a decade. She is a listening ear when things are a mess and wise counsel when my kids are up to no good. She has been used by God to bless us beyond belief. Her generosity has been instrumental in seeing some God-sized dreams come true for my husband and I. "Grace" walks through life with me and I would have missed it all if I had continued to believe the lies the enemy told me, held on to the baggage and remained at odds with her in my heart.

What is waiting for you on the other side of obedience, forgiveness and healing? I can tell you, first hand, there are much better things ahead than anything you're holding onto now. Consequences await our sin but blessing awaits our obedience.

> *"Do not be deceived: God is not mocked, for what-*
> *ever one sows, that will she also reap."*
> *~ Galatians 6:7*

I Wish I Had Known...

...That being consumed with what others think of me more than what God thinks of me is...SIN.

"I wish I could have understood the following concept at a younger age:

> *"If I am constantly looking sideways and comparing*
> *myself with my friend, my sister, my neighbor, or*
> *even a woman of another country, chances are I*

will be miserable. If I have more confidence in the
horizontal dimension of what others think than in the
vertical dimension of what God thinks,
then it is as if I commit idolatry."
~ *Ingrid Trobish, The Confident Woman*

Whoa. Idolatry? I was surprised by the use of that particular word, idolatry, but the Holy Spirit made it immediately clear it was indeed that serious. I had been guilty of idolatry for a long time. Comparing myself to other women and occupying my thoughts of how I looked in comparison . . . my hair, my clothes, my singing, my marriage, my voice, and most of all my body. The Lord began to show me, and constantly remind me, it is the heart He is concerned with and our only comparison should be done by looking in His face.

How do our thoughts, our speech, our demeanor, our time spent, our actions compare to Him?

Now, don't misunderstand, me. I have not spent the last 15 (plus) years since then basking in His presence without another sideways glance. Certainly not. He has to remind me over and over again where my eyes need to be fixed. And now, as I raise my daughter, the reality and the gravity of this truth is daily in my thoughts as I watch her interact with her young girl friends. My prayer is that her only source of confidence and identity will be in knowing who she is in Christ.

~ Tara Root

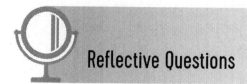

Reflective Questions

- What is the biggest consequence I've experienced due to any of the "spoilers" that have been discussed in this book?

Section 4

WHAT HAPPENS WHEN WE GET ALONG

CHAPTER 18
The End Game (Unity)

"Sisters, we were made for kindness
We can pierce the darkness as He shines through us
We will come reaching, with a song of healing
And they will know us by our love"
~ Christy Nockels

You Have an Enemy, and it's Not *Her*

When you are tempted to heap all the blame on another woman, remember that although it can feel that way, she is not your enemy. An enticing world system, our own sinful nature and Satan's active agents are all focused on relentlessly dividing us. Past trauma or drama, hurts or emotional pain can distort our perception like a scratched pair of sunglasses. The world and our flesh can destroy even the best of relationships. Left unchecked, our flesh will fight against God (Galatians 5:17), against fellow sisters in Christ (James 4:1) and against our own well being (Romans 8:6-8). We must, however, also be aware of the master manipulator. Satan has an army of operatives who twist our views of who is to blame and he will do anything he can to divide us.

When unity is disrupted, I encourage you to take a close look within to see what is really happening. Is your old nature projecting blame and contributing to your problem? Has Satan gained a foothold (Ephesians 27) that he is using to create division? It is crucial that we allow the Holy Spirit to direct our lives and help us towards unity, or we will constantly live divided and in defeat.

There have been nights I've tossed and turned and stewed and sighed over something another woman has said or done to me. I am willing to bet you've done the same. The next morning, even if *I'm* over it, my head still isn't over it, and I'm certainly not firing on all cylinders.

And, that's exactly how the enemy hopes you function - *not firing on all cylinders.*

You see, Satan wants us weak, frustrated, distracted and divided. When we allow wounds to fester, words to take hold and hurts to hang on, he's got us right where he wants us: weighed down, distracted, divided and ineffective.

Our enemy knows that we're a powerful force, ladies. He knows what we can do when we work together, when *we get along.* He also knows how to dig his dirty fingernails into situations making us believe it's actually *her* dirty fingernails that are digging into *us.* But it's not always. So often, it's him. The father of lies is conniving and he uses other people to do his dirty work. He's a master puppeteer pulling the strings, and the gal who gets your goat is simply his puppet. He plays us like a fiddle. He is behind the battles and the drama.

Girlfriends, it's not her - it's *him*.

The powerful and insightful Priscilla Shirer has got it figured out too. She sees right through him and she understands how he manipulates us:

"If I were your enemy, I'd work to create division between you and other Christians, between groups of Christians, anyone with the potential for uniting in battle against me and my plans. I'd keep you operating individually, not seeing your need for the church or tying yourself too closely to its mission. Strength in numbers and unity of purpose...I would not allow things like these to go unchecked."[15] ~ Fervent

Priscilla likens our battles with one another to that of "friendly fire". But, there is nothing friendly about it!

"When it happens in these circles, it's no accident. Friendly fire in the church or in our most vital relationships is almost always code for enemy activity. He knows his odds of success jump markedly whenever he can cause heart wrenching division between us, isolate one or two of us, and separate us into warring stonewalled camps."[16] ~ Fervent

We have *got* to recognize that the one who's causing us problems isn't always the one we can see with our own two eyes. He's much smarter than that. He's figured out how to make us shoot our wounded, but it's time we band together and fight back. It is time we fight fire with fire.

Fire Hazards and Body Builders

All over scripture we see The Lord described as fire. Hebrews 12:29 calls Him a *"consuming fire"*. This is not just a metaphor. God *will* consume, devour and put away darkness and evil for good one day soon. In the meantime, He gives us the power to ward off the evil one, using His word and His tactics.

We are strong when we stick together. There is power in numbers. We know this. We'd never let our children venture into dangerous territory alone, so why should we? God's word tells us that we are fierce when we are fused together; a body ready for battle. Ephesians 4:16 tells us:

"He makes the whole body fit together perfectly.
As each part does its own special work, it helps the
other parts grow, so that the whole body is healthy
and growing and full of love."

A whole, healthy body is our best battle plan. When we function as God intended, in *unity*, our chances of victory increase. This means we forego cutting each other off and out of the picture. We put the claws away and begin to work together.

We need to stick together. We aren't meant to be divided, just like the paper dolls on the cover aren't either. Unified is how we were meant to be. We are much, much stronger together.

Room Enough

Too many of us have been competing when we should be coalescing. The body of Christ is big and there's always room to grow. There is *room enough* for us all. We are *all* needed in order to keep that body healthy, active and victorious. Whatever part you play, you are important and valued. You are needed. Don't try to be something you were not intended to be, and please don't prevent another woman in doing the same. We function best and find our meaning when we function how we were made - to *work together*. Listen to The Message's take on Romans 12:4-6:

> *"In this way we are like the various parts of a human body. Each part gets its meaning from the body as a whole, not the other way around. The body we're talking about is Christ's body of chosen people. Each of us finds our meaning and function as a part of his body. But as a chopped-off finger or cut-off toe we wouldn't amount to much, would we?*
>
> *So since we find ourselves fashioned into all these excellently formed and marvelously functioning parts in Christ's body, let's just go ahead and be what we were made to be, without enviously or pridefully comparing ourselves with each other, or trying to be something we aren't."*

Do you see how, when we unify, the body is better for it and we cause *Christ* to shine? This is our end game. This is how we *all* win.

Why *Should* we Get Along?

I'll admit I've asked myself the same question during moments of weakness: "Why *should* we get along!?" I mean, who even cares anyway?

I've had all the supposed arguments and excuses for not getting along in my back pocket:

"She just won't cooperate with me... "

"She's just different... "

"I've tried..."

"We'll never see eye to eye..."

"She's just not the type of girl I'd enjoy..."

"She's dangerous..."

"I can't compete..."

"I'm out of her league..."

"She's out of my league..."

"We can just coexist..."

"Remember how she treated me..."

Sound familiar?

It's in times like this that my loving Father quickly reminds me, *"Your love for one another will prove to the world that you are my disciples."* ~ John 13:35 (NLT)

When we can't figure out how to love one another, the world won't want to love Jesus, plain and simple. But, when we let go and let God handle our emotions and our relationships, we not only help ourselves, we save a dying world.

> *"Authentic Community is the most powerful apologetic on the face of the Earth. It's the greatest need among Christians and the greatest need for an unbelieving world to begin to believe that what we say about Jesus is true because of how we love and relate to one another...When we radically and authentically love one another from the heart, the world stands back in awe and wonders, "What makes them care so deeply for one another?"* [23]
> *~ Chip Ingram, True Spirituality*

So, ladies, let's connect our fragile selves, stick together and be an avalanche of love. The world is watching and waiting for us to *get along.*

> *"Snowflakes are one of nature's most fragile things, but just look what they can do when they stick together." ~ Vista M. Kelly*

CHAPTER 19
Blessings of Getting Along

We now know some consequences of *not* getting along. I want you to hear first hand from women the blessings they've enjoyed when they "get along" God's way. These are awesome, and exactly how the body of Christ should function:

> *"Every Wednesday a group of us women and our daughters rally together to knit dolls for African children who are sick or injured and in the hospital. They become the packing protection for medical supplies instead of styrofoam peanuts and they get to keep them!"*

> *"A week after I had my first baby, a sweet lady from our church called to ask how she could help me. Since many others were already bringing meals, she insisted she come help me clean the house. Since I was too sore and too tired, I accepted her generous offer. Not only did she do my dishes, she cleaned my bathroom! Tears rolled down my cheeks as I laid in my bed holding my newborn, listening to her scrub my dirty tub and floors. And ladies, this wasn't just*

any dirty bathroom - this was the bathroom of a woman who had just given birth. That was a true act of love I will always remember, and have actually passed on to a friend of mine after she delivered. Us women need to stick together! We need each other!"

"When I was going through my separation and divorce, my friend really helped me. I loved it when she would say to me..."Stressed? Nah. You're just blessed because God is carrying you through this mess."

"I can honestly say, had I not had the positive, godly women role models in my life throughout the years, I wouldn't be where I am today. Having these women speak into my life and provide words of encouragement and affirmation made all the difference when I felt down and defeated."

"Things amazing women have said to me:

'You are a force to be reckoned with!'
(Which made me feel powerful!)

'I don't know how you do it, I'm always bragging to people about you.'
(From a dear friend, amazing in her own right)

'You always spoil me.'

(I had no idea I was spoiling. I was just showing love in a time I knew she needed it)"

"I have a friend who has shown me such faithfulness in friendship it is hard to write about her without crying lol! She challenges me to invest in relationships and love others even when it's not convenient. She has proven to be a friend who encourages me, speaks the truth in love, and pursues nurturing our friendship, even when it's not convenient for her. She has chosen to stay a part of my life when she didn't have to - my family and I moved two states away and she pursued our friendship even across the miles to make sure we stayed connected. Through our adult years of change - marriages, kids, job craziness, and geographical distance - Sarah has showed me how to be a friend when it takes work. She has exemplified to me what investing in relationships looks like, and because of that we have a friendship that is stronger than ever!"

"Words of wisdom from women in my life definitely formed who I am today. It helped to have those words ringing in my ears when it came to making certain decisions. I knew which one was right and which one was not. To know that someone truly wanted to see me grow and succeed mattered to me. The person I am today is a result of them sowing seeds in my life. These women pushed me to do hard and great things."

"I have issues with my self worth and feeling beautiful. I am married to an unbelieving husband who de-values me. My friend gave me a mug that says "Good Morning Beautiful'. Every time I use it I smile. And I'm actually starting to believe it. This same friend makes time for me. That in itself is such a gift!"

"My mom was my most positive role model in my life. She taught me kindness and how to help others. She helped me have a heart for the underdog, the unloved and the unwanted. She had such an impact on me."

"My best friends and I don't live near each other right now, so we make a point to voice text through-out the week to stay connected. It's a little more personal than a regular text! I can't tell you the number of times I've received a prayer, a song or just a little hello that was exactly what I needed to hear."

"I received a note out of the blue from a friend who said she hoped I was doing well and she appreciated our friendship. When we talked, even if we were sharing about our struggles, she liked how I was able to find something positive out of the conversation and lift her spirit. That note was super encouraging because I was feeling really isolated and discouraged personally at the time."

"Over the years, I have felt loved and encouraged by 'just because' gifts from friends. They are usually not expensive, but often thoughtful. (And lately, kinda funny!) The gifts say, 'I know you, and I thought of you'. Makes my heart smile."

"There were a couple ladies in my life who really impacted me when they told me the truth - even when I didn't want to hear it. It was with love and grace, and it changed the course of my life."

It is clear to see that, although we can feel weak and insignificant at times, when we link arms like those delicate paper dolls you're holding, or unify like those tiny snowflakes and "stick together", we become stronger. Then, we can offer strength to each other. I am not perfect but I am a work in progress. I know you are too. When we choose *His* ways, we will become women who reflect His image and fight for each other, rather than *against* one another. It will be *then* that the enemy doesn't stand a fighting chance against us.

*"May our dependably steady and warmly personal God develop maturity in you so that you **get along** with each other as well as Jesus gets along with us all. Then we'll be a choir - not our voices only, but our very lives singing in harmony in a stunning anthem to the God and Father of our Master Jesus!"*
~ Romans 15:1-7 (MSG) (emphasis mine)

Section 5
Recipes

Some of my Favorite Women Share Their Favorite Recipes!

My blog (**frommilktomeat.com**) provides you with many of my favorite, tried and true recipes. I am now going to bestow on you a wonderful collection of recipes from some of my favorite tried and true women throughout the years! The most fun item I crossed off my book "to-do" list was testing all of these recipes out. Ladies, you're in for a treat!

Thank you to all my friends and family members who contributed to this, and thank you for your contribution in my life. You have made it much sweeter!

Breakfast

Ann's Carrot Pineapple Muffins

- 1 C white sugar (may replace 1/2 C Stevia)
- 2/3 C oil
- 2 lg eggs, beaten
- 1 1/2 C all purpose flour
- 2 tsp baking powder
- 1 tsp baking soda
- 1 1/2 tsp cinnamon
- 1/2 tsp salt
- 1 tsp vanilla
- 1 C finely grated carrot (1 lg)
- 1 C canned crushed pineapple, drained

In beater bowl, combine sugar, oil and beaten eggs. In another bowl, combine flour, baking powder, baking soda, cinnamon and salt and mix well. Add dry ingredients to the sugar and oil mixture and stir to moisten. Add grated carrots, pineapple and vanilla. Fill greased muffin cups to the top and bake at 375 degrees for 20 minutes. Yields 9-10 large muffins.

~ Ann Mainse

Banana Muffins

- 3 bananas, mashed
- ⅔ C white sugar
- 1 egg
- ½ C flour
- 1 tsp baking soda
- 1 tsp baking powder
- ½ tsp salt
- ¼ C shortening or oil

Mix until moistened and spoon into greased muffin tins. Bake 20 mins at 350 degrees.

~ Emily Friday *(Original recipe, Aunt Nancy Gatten)*

Avocado Toast Spread

- 1 Avocado
- Dash of sea salt
- Dash of pepper
- 1 tsp crushed red pepper
- 1 tsp onion powder
- 1 tsp minced onion

Cut up avocado into chunks, then stir everything together until creamy. Spread on your favorite toast! We use sprouted grain Ezekiel bread.

~ Monica Orzechowski

Orange Nut Loaf

- 2 1/2 C flour
- 1 C sugar
- 3 1/2 tsp baking powder
- 1/4 tsp. powdered ginger
- 1 tsp Salt
- 3 Tbsp oil
- 1/2 C milk
- 1 1/2 Tbsp grated orange rind
- 3/4 cup orange juice
- 1 egg
- 1 cup finely chopped nuts

Preheat oven to 350 degrees. Grease and flour a 9x5x3" loaf pan. Measure ingredients into a bowl. Scraping bowl constantly, beat with mixer at medium speed for half a minute. Pour into pan.

Bake 55 to 65 minutes or until loaf tests done. Remove from pan & cool thoroughly before slicing.

~ Judy Bodaly

Gluten Free, Dairy Free, Banana Bread

- 1 1 ¼ C of each:
    - » Almond Meal
    - » Quick Oats
    - » Bob's Red Mill Pancake mix
- Dash of cinnamon

Mix these ingredients together in a bowl and set aside

In another bowl, mix together:

- 1 egg
- ¼ C granulated sugar
- ¼ C brown sugar
- 2-3 Tbsp pure maple syrup
- 3 Tbsp coconut oil, melted
- ½ tsp vanilla
- 3 ½ tsp baking powder
- ¾ tsp sea salt
- ¾ C almond milk
- 3 ripe bananas, mashed

Mix above ingredients together. Stir in dry flour mixture. Put into a greased loaf pan and bake in a preheated 350 degree oven for 1 hour and 15 minutes.

~ Lori Lorenze

Ham and Eggs Brunch Braid

- 4 ounces cream cheese
- 1/2 cup milk
- 8 eggs, divided
- 1/4 teaspoon salt
- Dash ground black pepper
- 1/4 cup red bell pepper, chopped
  (~or~ Cherry Red Tomatoes quartered)
- 2 tablespoons sliced green onions with tops
- 1 teaspoon butter or margarine
- 2 packages (8 ounces each) refrigerated crescent rolls
- 1/4 pound diced deli ham
- 1/2 cup (2 ounces) shredded cheddar cheese

Preheat oven to 375° F. Place cream cheese and milk in bowl. Microwave on HIGH 1 minute. Whisk until smooth. Separate 1 egg, reserve egg white. Add the yolk and remaining 7 eggs, salt and black pepper to batter bowl; whisk to combine.

Chop bell pepper or use red cherry tomatoes cut up in quarters. Add ham, bell pepper/tomatoes and onions to egg mixture. Melt butter in non stick cook pan (do not use stainless cookware) over medium-low heat. Add egg mixture; cook, stirring occasionally, until eggs are set but still moist. Remove pan from heat.

Unroll 1 package of crescent dough; do not separate. Arrange longest side of dough across width of rectangle Stone. Repeat with remaining package of dough. Press dough together to seal perforations. On longest sides of baking Stone, cut dough into strips 1 1/2 inches apart, 3 inches deep (there will be 6 inches in the center for the filling). Spread shredded cheddar cheese over eggs. To braid, lift strips of dough across filling to meet in center, twisting each strip one turn. Continue alternating strips to form a braid.

Brush lightly beaten egg white over dough using a basting brush. Bake 25-28 minutes or until deep golden brown. Cut into slices along the braid.

~ Jeannette Willis
(Based upon an original Pampered Chef Recipe)

Appetizers

Goat Cheese and Baguette Appetizer

Thinly slice a long baguette of your choice.

Toss the slices in a bowl with evoo and some basil and/or oregano until lightly coated.

Arrange them on a baking sheet in a single layer.

In the middle of that same baking sheet, place an entire package of goat cheese that you have formed into a ball. If you so choose, you can lightly coat it with oil and crushed pecans.

Bake at 350F until baguette slices are toasted and goat cheese is softening.

To eat, take a baguette slice, slather some goat cheese on top and then add a dollop of fresh salsa (optional).

~ Diane Gale

Young Onion Tart with Cantal, Applewood smoked bacon and Herb Salad (Aka - Amazing Pizza!)

- 1 sheet frozen all-butter puff pastry
- 2 extra-large egg yolks
- ½-pound slab applewood smoked bacon
- 2 tablespoons extra virgin olive oil
- 2 cups sliced young onions, red and white if possible
- 1 tablespoon thyme leaves
- ½ cup diagonally sliced young onion tops
- ½ cup whole milk ricotta, drained if wet
- ¼ cup creme fraiche
- 1/3 pound Cantal, Gruyère, or Comté cheese, thinly sliced
- ½ cup flat-leaf parsley leaves
- ¼ cup tarragon leaves
- ¼ cup chervil sprigs (french parsley)
- ¼ cup 1/2-inch-snipped chives
- A drizzle super-good extra virgin olive oil
- ½ lemon, for juicing
- Kosher salt and freshly ground black pepper

Preheat the oven to 400°F. Defrost the puff pastry slightly and unroll it onto a parchment-lined baking sheet. Use a paring knife to score a 1/4-inch border around the edge of the pastry.

Make an egg wash by whisking one egg yolk with 1/2 teaspoon water, and brush the egg wash along the border. (You will not need all of the egg wash.)

Return the puff pastry to the freezer until you're ready to use it.

Slice the bacon into 3/8-inch-thick slices. Stack the slices in two piles, then cut the bacon crosswise into 3/8-inch even-sided rectangles or lardons.

Heat a large sauté pan over high heat for 2 minutes. Add 1 tablespoon olive oil, and allow to heat another minute.

Add the bacon, and sauté over medium high heat 4 to 5 minutes, until slightly crisp but still tender. Reduce the heat to low, and toss in the young onions, thyme, and 1/2 teaspoon salt. Stir together a minute or two, until the onions are just wilted. Toss in the onion tops, and remove to a baking sheet or platter to cool.

Place the ricotta, remaining egg yolk, and remaining table-spoon olive oil in the bowl of a food processor. Purée until smooth, and transfer to a medium bowl.

Gently fold in the crème fraîche and season with 1/8 tea-spoon salt and a pinch of pepper.

Spread the ricotta mixture on the puff pastry within the scored border. Lay the Cantal over the ricotta, and arrange the bacon-onion mixture on top.

Bake the tart 20 to 25 minutes, rotating the baking sheet once, until the cheese is bubbling and the crust is golden brown. Lift up the edge of the tart and peek underneath to make sure the crust is cooked through. (If you underbake the tart, it will be soggy.)

Toss the herbs in a small bowl with salt, pepper, a drizzle of super-good olive oil, and a squeeze of lemon juice.

Let the tart cool a few minutes, and serve it on a cutting board at the table. Serve the herb salad in a small, pretty bowl.

To serve individual portions, cut six wedges from the tart and garnish each one with a little herb salad.

~ Tara Root (*Original Recipe, Suzanne Goin, cookstr.com*)

Buffalo Chicken Wing Dip

- 2 chicken breasts
- 1 jar blue cheese dip
- ½ C Frank's hot sauce
- 3 C shredded cheddar cheese
- 2 bricks cream cheese at room temperature

Boil chicken, cool and then shred or dice into small pieces. Mix remaining ingredients well in a large bowl and then combine chicken.

Pour into glass baking dish and bake 30-40 minutes at 350 degrees, or until brown and bubbly.

Once cooled a bit, serve warm with tortilla or pita chips, carrot and celery sticks.

~ Jodi Guilmette

Lunch / Salads

Gluten and Sugar Free Wraps

- ¼ C almond flour
- ¼ C + 1 tbsp tapioca flour
- 1/2 tsp salt
- ½ tsp xylitol

Whisk ingredients together. Add warm water until thin (like pancake batter). Pour over a hot, olive oiled iron skillet. Add salt and pepper to taste while cooking.

Allow it to rise and bubble. Flip a couple of times. You may need to add a bit of oil.

Makes one simple, pliable, gluten/sugar free wrap.

~ Robin Cleugh

Greek Quinoa Salad

- 3 Tbsp freshly squeezed lemon juice
- 1 Tbsp red wine vinegar
- 1/4 tsp dried oregano
- 1 clove garlic, smashed and finely chopped to a paste
- Kosher salt and freshly ground black pepper
- 1/4 C extra-virgin olive oil
- 1 C quinoa
- 2 C red and yellow grape tomatoes, halved
- 1 C pitted kalamata olives
- 2 green onions (green & pale green part), thinly sliced
- 2 pickled cherry peppers, diced
- 1 small red onion, halved and thinly sliced
- 1/2 English cucumber, cut into small dice
- Feta, for sprinkling

Directions

Whisk together the lemon juice, vinegar, oregano, garlic and some salt and pepper in a small bowl. Slowly whisk in the oil until emulsified. Let sit at room temperature while you prepare the salad to allow the flavors to meld.

Rinse the quinoa in a strainer until the water runs clear. Combine the quinoa, 2 cups water, 1 teaspoon salt and 1/4 teaspoon pepper in a small saucepan, bring to a boil and cook until the water is absorbed and the quinoa is tender, about 15 minutes.

Transfer to a bowl, fluff with a fork and let sit for 5 minutes to cool slightly.

Add the tomatoes, olives, green onions, cherry peppers, red onions, cucumbers and dressing and toss to coat. Cover and refrigerate for at least 1 hour and up to 8 hours before serving. The longer it sits the better the flavor.

Just before serving, transfer to a platter and sprinkle feta on top.

~ Sarah King
(Original recipe Bobby Flay, Food Network Website)

Super Summer Kale Salad

- 3/4 cup white sugar
- 1/2 cup vinegar
- 1/2 teaspoon salt
- 1/2 teaspoon ground black pepper
- 1/4 cup extra-virgin olive oil
- 1 bunch kale, stems removed and leaves chopped
- 16 ounces frozen shelled edamame, thawed (soybeans)
- 1/4 red onion, sliced thin
- 1 cup shredded carrot
- 2/3 cup fresh blueberries
- 1/2 cup dried sweetened cranberries
- 1/2 cup cashew pieces
- 1/2 cup shelled roasted sunflower seeds

Whisk sugar, vinegar, salt, pepper, and olive oil together in a bowl until sugar is dissolved; set aside. Toss kale, edamame, red onion, carrot, blueberries, dried cranberries, cashew pieces, and sunflower seeds together in a bowl. Pour about half the dressing over the mixture and toss to coat. Cover bowl with plastic wrap and refrigerate 4 to 6 hours. Serve remaining dressing on side.

~ Sandra Milby

Summer Fresh Salad

- Romaine and/or baby spinach or Muslin mix
- Tin of mandarin oranges
- 1 pint of Strawberries
- 2 Kiwi
- ¾ C Slivered toasted almonds (toast at 350 for 5 min)

Dressing:
- 1/2 cup vinegar
- 1/2 cup oil
- 1/2 cup sugar
- 1 tsp salt

Wash your greens mix of choice, wash and slice strawberries, peel and slice kiwi, toast the almonds and then toss together. Whisk dressing ingredients together and toss salad with dressing just before serving.

~ Kerri McLeod

Tuscan Roasted Butternut Squash & Kale

- ½ tsp Tuscan Seasoning
- 1 Tbsp olive oil, divided
- 1 medium red onion, peeled, 1 inch dice
- ½ 16 oz pkg kale greens.
- 1 Butternut squash cut into chunks
- Salt & pepper to taste

Preheat oven to 350 degrees. Add Tuscan seasoning and 1 ½ Tbsp oil in a large bowl; mix to combine. Add squash & onions. Toss to coat. Arrange squash & onions in a single layer on baking sheet. Roast 30 min, remove from oven. Toss kale with remaining oil; season with salt & pepper. Add kale to pan with veggies; toss lightly to combine. Roast another 30 min, until brown and tender. Season with salt & pepper; serve.

~ Rebecca O'Hara

Dinner

Spaghetti Carbonara

- 8 ounces spaghetti
- 2 large eggs
- 1/2 cup freshly grated parmesan
- 4 slices bacon, diced
- 4 cloves garlic, minced
- Kosher salt and freshly ground black pepper, to taste
- 2 tbsp chopped fresh parsley leaves

In a large pot of boiling salted water, cook pasta according to package instructions; reserve 1/2 cup water and drain well. In a small bowl, whisk together eggs and Parmesan; set aside.

Heat a large skillet over medium high heat. Add bacon and cook until brown and crispy, about 6-8 minutes; reserve excess fat. Stir in garlic until fragrant, about 1 minute. Reduce heat to low. Working quickly, stir in pasta and egg mixture, and gently toss to combine; season with salt and pepper, to taste. Add reserved pasta water, one tablespoon at a time, until desired consistency is reached. Serve immediately, garnished with parsley, if desired.

~ Hannah Lukings

Dr. McDougall's Red Veggie Burgers

- 15 ounce can black beans, drained and rinsed
- 1/2 C cooked, chilled brown rice
- 1/4 C fat-free barbecue sauce
- 1/4 C quick cooking oats
- 1/4 C dried whole wheat bread crumbs
- 1/4 C diced fresh mushrooms
- 2 Tbsp minced canned beets
- 2 Tbsp minced golden raisins
- 1 Tbsp minced onion
- 1 tsp minced garlic
- 1 tsp chili powder
- 1/4 tsp cumin
- Several twists freshly ground black pepper
- Dash sea salt

Glaze:
- 2 Tbsp soy sauce
- 2 Tbsp hoisin sauce
- 1 Tbsp molasses

Mix all the ingredients for the burgers in a large bowl, slightly mashing the beans while stirring the mixture together. Let rest for 10 minutes.

Combine the ingredients for the glaze in a separate bowl and set aside.

Form the burger mixture into 6 patties. Mixture will be moist and easy to form into patties. (May be placed on a platter, covered and refrigerated at this point.)

Place on a pre-heated non-stick griddle and cook for several minutes on each side, flipping occasionally until lightly browned and cooked through.

Brush with the glaze after the final flip and grill an additional minute. Brush the remaining glaze on both sides of toasted whole wheat buns, and serve with lettuce, tomato slices and sliced sweet onion, if desired.

~ Stephanie Koch

Chicken Wings

- 1/2 C soya sauce
- 1/2 C orange marmalade
- 1/2 C ground ginger
- 1/4 C garlic powder

Mix the ingredients. Dip rinsed and patted dry, split chicken wings. Coat thoroughly with marinade and lay in shallow broiling pan. (No rack)

Bake at 350 degrees for 1 hour. Turn after 1/2 hour.

~ Peggy Macaulay

Crockpot Salsa Chicken

- 3 Chicken breasts
- 1 Jar salsa
- 1 can black beans
- 1 can corn
- ½ brick of cream cheese

Cook all together in crockpot (except cream cheese) for 4 hours on high, or 8 hours on low.

During the last hour, add cream cheese and stir. Finish cooking.

Cheddar cheese is a nice addition to this recipe, and you may serve as chili or with chips or fresh greens.

~ Terri Kelly

Creamy Parmesan Garlic Mushroom Chicken

- ◆ 4 boneless, skinless chicken breasts, thinly sliced
- ◆ 2 Tbsp Olive oil
- ◆ Salt Pepper
- ◆ 8 oz sliced mushrooms

Creamy Parmesan Garlic Sauce:

- ◆ ¼ C butter
- ◆ 2 garlic cloves, minced
- ◆ 1 tablespoon flour
- ◆ ½ C chicken broth
- ◆ 1 C heavy cream or half and half
- ◆ ½ C grated parmesan cheese
- ◆ ½ teaspoon garlic powder
- ◆ ¼ teaspoon pepper
- ◆ ½ teaspoon salt
- ◆ 1 C spinach, chopped

In a large skillet add olive oil and cook the chicken on medium high heat for 3-5 minutes on each side or until brown on each side and cooked until no longer pink in center. Remove chicken and set aside on a plate.

Add the sliced mushrooms and cook for a few minutes until tender. Remove and set aside.

To make the sauce add the butter and melt. Add garlic and

cook until tender. Whisk in the flour until it thickens. Whisk in chicken broth, heavy cream, parmesan cheese, garlic powder, pepper and salt.

Add the spinach and let simmer until it starts to thicken and spinach wilts. Add the chicken and mushrooms back to the sauce and serve over pasta if desired

~ Sarah Auger *(original recipe, Alyssa Rivers)*

Slow Cooker Sweet and Spicy Chicken

- ◆ 3 lbs boneless, skinless chicken thighs
- ◆ 1 red bell pepper, seeded and sliced
- ◆ 1 yellow bell pepper, seeded and sliced
- ◆ 3 C broccoli florets

For the Sauce

- ◆ 2 C apricot jam
- ◆ 2 cloves garlic, minced
- ◆ 2 tbsp soy sauce or coconut aminos
- ◆ 2 tbsp dry mustard
- ◆ 2 tsp dried minced onion
- ◆ 2 tsp sea salt
- ◆ ½ tsp ground ginger
- ◆ ½ tsp red pepper flakes (or more for a spicier sauce)
- ◆ 2 tbsp arrowroot powder (optional)

Cut chicken thighs into bite sized chunks and place in slow cooker. Cut the veggies as noted above. Place in bowl and refrigerate until ready to use.

In medium bowl, whisk together the jam, garlic, soy sauce or coconut aminos, mustard, onion, salt, ginger and red pepper flakes. Pour over the chicken. Cover and cook on low for 4 to 5 hours.

Check the chicken at the 4 hour mark. If not cooked through, continue cooking. Once chicken is cooked through, add bell peppers and broccoli florets.

Continue cooking on low until veggies are al dente. Use a slotted spoon to remove chicken and veggies from slow cooker and place in a serving dish.

Whisk in arrowroot powder to thicken sauce if desired. To serve, ladle sauce over chicken and veggies and serve with rice or cauli-rice.

~ Cindy Lezynski

Soup

Creamy Tuscan Garlic Tortellini Soup

- 2 Tablespoons butter
- 1 small white onion, diced
- 3 cloves garlic, minced
- 4 cups chicken broth
- 28 ounce can diced tomatoes
- 1 15 ounce can white beans, drained and rinsed
- 1 cup heavy cream
- ¼ cup grated parmesan cheese
- 1 Tablespoon italian seasoning
- 1 teaspoon salt
- ¼ teaspoon pepper
- 2 cups cooked and shredded chicken (I used rotisserie)
- 9 ounce refrigerated tortellini
- 2 cups spinach

In a large pot over medium heat, heat up the butter. Add onion and garlic and cook until tender. Add chicken broth, diced tomatoes, white beans, heavy cream, parmesan cheese, italian seasoning, salt and pepper. Bring to a simmer.

Add the chicken, tortellini, and spinach. Let simmer for 10 minutes to thicken up and for the tortellini to cook.

~ Kaylee Strozyk

Taco Soup

- 1 lb lean ground beef
- 1 small onion, chopped
- 1 15 oz can kidney beans, undrained
- 1 15 oz can black beans, undrained
- 1 15 oz can corn kernels, undrained
- 1 15 oz can diced tomatoes
- 1 8 oz can tomato sauce
- 1 pkg (2 tbsp) taco seasoning

Optional Toppings

- Shredded cheddar cheese
- Sour cream
- Diced tomato / pico de gallo
- Sliced avocado
- Corn chips
- Lime wedges
- Chopped cilantro

Brown the ground beef and onions in a large pot until cooked through and crumbled. Drain excess fat. Add the remaining ingredients to the pot and stir to combine.

Cook over medium heat, letting simmer for about 10 minutes to let flavors blend. Serve with optional toppings. Serves 4. Recipe may be doubled.

~ Karen Wood

Cauliflower Soup

- 1 head cauliflower, chopped
- 2 medium white potatoes, peeled and chopped
- ½ cooking onion, chopped
- 1 tsp salt and ¼ tsp pepper
- 1 C Shredded cheddar cheese
- Chives and cheddar cheese for garnish

- 50/50 water or stock & milk to cover veggies plus a little extra milk

Lightly boil until veggies are soft enough for blending, stirring often (it's milk after all) Once cooled, use immersion blender to make everything thick and creamy then dump cheese in, re-heat on low heat to melt cheese. I sometimes throw in a swirl of olive oil 'cause it never hurt. Serve with crusty bread.

You could fish out some of the cauliflower before blending and then add them back if you aren't trying to hide from kids what is in the soup. Add more milk if soup is too thick.

* *You can trick kids and call it potato-cheese soup. They'll never know!*

~ Carrie Escaf

Red Lentil CrockPot Soup

- 2 tablespoons extra virgin olive oil
- 1 large yellow onion, diced
- 3 celery stalks, diced
- 3 medium carrots, trimmed, peeled, and diced
- 2 medium zucchini, ends trimmed and chopped into 3/4-inch chunks
- 3 Yukon gold potatoes, scrubbed and chopped into 3/4-inch cubes
- 3/4 cup split red lentils
- 1 cup canned chopped tomatoes (with their juices)
- 2 dried bay leaves
- 3-4 sprigs of fresh thyme
- 5 cups chicken stock
- 1 teaspoon kosher sea salt, plus more
- black pepper
- 2-3 cups finely sliced savoy cabbage, reserved for later
- extra virgin olive oil, for drizzling
- fresh flat-leaf parsley (or basil), for garnishing
- freshly grated parmigiano-reggiano cheese, for garnishing

Add the following to the slow cooker (this recipe will fit a 4-quart capacity slow cooker): olive oil, onion, celery, carrot, zucchini, potatoes, split red lentils, chopped tomatoes, parmigiano rind, bay leaves, thyme, chicken stock, kosher salt, and black pepper. Stir together.

Cook on high heat for 4-6 hours, or until the red lentils are tender (or alternatively, cook on low heat for 8-10 hours). In the last hour of cook time (or 2 hours, if you are cooking over low heat), add the thinly sliced cabbage.

Remove and discard the dried bay leaves and any tough thyme sprigs. Adjust the seasoning to taste salt and pepper.

Serve the soup and top each serving with a drizzle of extra virgin olive oil, a sprinkle of freshly chopped parsley, and/ or freshly grated parmigiano-reggiano.

~ Lisa Littlewood (*original recipe www.abeautifulplate.com*)

Nat's Version of Scouse

- Any cooking oil
- diced chuck steak or stewing beef (can be made with lamb as a substitute for the beef)
- a few splashes of Worcester sauce
- diced onion
- 350g carrots (and any other veg you desire)
- 600g peeled and diced potatoes (cut into 1.5 cm cubes)
- A cup of Beer (optional)
- Beef or vegetable stock (I save water from any vegetables that I've boiled and then freeze it, that way I always have a stock on hand with no additives)
- Salt and pepper

The traditional way to make this (like my nana) is to boil all the ingredients together and then simmer all day. I've often been to my nan's house and had her mention how she has 'a pan of scouse on' cooking - a common thing to hear in a Liverpool home. I make mine slightly different and when my nana recently witnessed me cooking it, she was adamant that it wasn't 'Liverpool' scouse. That said, she still reluctantly admitted that it was tasty and she enjoyed it. This is a simple recipe that warms you on a cold day - perfect comfort food.

Fry up the beef in a little oil until browned. Add onions and carrots, Worcester sauce and salt and pepper. Add one potato and keep cooking until all the ingredients are soft.

Add stock and simmer for as long as possible (you can put it in a slow cooker at this point and go to work).

About 45 mins before serving, add potatoes, turn it backup to boil until the potatoes are cooked.

Serve with crusty bread and slices of beetroot.

~ Natalie Thompson

Corn Chowder

- 2 C chopped peeled potatoes
- 1/2 C thinly sliced carrots
- 1/2 C thinly sliced celery
- 1/4 C chopped onion
- 1/4 tsp plack pepper
- 1/4 C butter
- 1/4 C flour
- 2 C milk
- 1/2 cup parmesan cheese (you can use less to taste)
- 17 oz can of corn (I use frozen corn)

In a large pot stir two cups of water, potato, carrot, celery, onion and black pepper. Bring to a boil, reduce heat - cover and simmer for ten minutes.

In a large saucepan melt butter, stir in flour, add milk all at once. Cook and stir over medium heat until mixture is thickened and bubbly. Cook and stir for one minute more.

Add cheese stirring until it is melted. Carefully add cream to vegetable mixture. Add corn. Heat the soup through stirring occasionally. Do not boil.

~ Jen Quinton

Dessert

Peach and Raspberry Crisp

Fruit Layer
- 5 C peeled and sliced peaches
- 1 C raspberries
- 1/3 brown sugar
- 2 Tbsp flour

Topping
- 3/4 C of flour
- 3/4 C of quick oats
- 3/4 brown sugar
- 1/2 teaspoon cinnamon
- 1/2 teaspoon ground ginger
- 1/2 C of soft (or melted butter)

Fill an 8 inch glass baking dish with peeled and sliced peaches. Add the raspberries and toss with 1/3 cup of brown sugar and 2 tbsp of flour. In a separate bowl combine the flour, quick oats, brown sugar, cinnamon, and ground ginger. Add butter and mix well. Crumble topping over fruit in baking dish and bake in a 350F oven for 45 minutes or until fruit is bubbly and cooked through.

This recipe is pretty forgiving and you can play with the amounts to suit your taste or the size of dish you are using.

~ Michelle Jones

Upside-down Fudge Brownie Pudding

- 1 C flour
- 2 tsp baking powder
- ¾ C sugar
- 3 tbsp cocoa
- ½ C milk
- 2 tbsp butter, melted
- 1 tsp vanilla
- ¼ C chopped walnuts (optional)
- ¾ C packed brown sugar
- 2 tbsp cocoa
- 2 C boiling water.

Grease slow cooker insert. In a large bowl, combine flour, baking powder, sugar and 3 tbsp cocoa. Mix well. In another bowl, combine milk, butter and vanilla.

Stir into flour mixture and add walnuts. The batter will be very thick. Spread evenly in prepared slow cooker insert.

In a bowl, combine brown sugar and 2 tbsp cocoa. Add boiling water, mixing well. Pour over batter in slow cooker. Cover and cook on high for 2 hours or until toothpick in center comes out clean. Spoon into individual bowls and serve with vanilla ice cream.

~ Wendy Pauls

Cookie Fruit Bars

Bars
- 2 pkgs sugar cookie mix
- 1 can pie filling of choice (raspberry is my favorite)

Glaze
- 1 C powdered sugar
- 1 tsp almond extract
- 2 tbsp milk or water (to start)

Make the first package of cookie mix according to the directions on the package. Grease a 9x13 pan. Press the prepared cookie dough into the bottom of the pan. Spread the pie filling over the cookie dough.

Make the second package of cookie mix according to directions on package. Crumble the cookie dough over the pie filling in little pieces.

Bake at 375 degrees for 25 minutes or until golden around the edges (I like mine a little under done). Mix glaze ingredients together and pour over the hot cookie bars and let them cool.

~ Kelly Jankowski

Chocolate Zucchini Cake

- 2 C all-purpose flour
- 2 C white sugar
- 3/4 C unsweetened cocoa powder
- 2 teaspoons baking soda
- 1 teaspoon baking powder
- 1/2 teaspoon salt
- 1 teaspoon ground cinnamon
- 4 eggs
- 1 1/2 C vegetable oil
- 3 C grated zucchini
- 3/4 C chopped walnuts

Preheat oven to 350 degrees F (175 degrees C). Grease and flour a 9x13 inch baking pan.

In a medium bowl, stir together the flour, sugar, cocoa, baking soda, baking powder, salt and cinnamon. Add the eggs and oil, mix well.

Fold in the nuts and zucchini until they are evenly distributed. Pour into the prepared pan.

Bake for 50 to 60 minutes in the preheated oven, until a knife inserted into the center comes out clean. Cool cake completely before frosting with your favorite frosting.

~ Shannon Ford (*Original Recipe, Sandy, allrecipes.com*)

Notes

1   Catrina Welch, *Confident Beauty*, (Morgan James Publishing 2014) p. 82

2   Jen Hatmaker, *Interrupted*, (http://goodreads.com/work/quotes/6386564-interrupted-an-adventure-in-relearning-the-essentials-of-faith)

3   June Hunt, *Jealousy and Envy*, (Hendrickson Publishers 2018) p. 19

4   Dr. Meg Meeker, *10 Habits of Happy Mothers*, (Ballantine Books 2011) p. 83

5   Bertrand Russel (http//en.wikipedia.org/wiki/Envy

6   Beth Moore, *So Long Insecurity* (Tyndale House, 2010) p. 286

7   http://mattmcwilliams.com/divorce-proof-marriage

8   Donald Miller, *Scary Close* (Thomas Nelson 2015) p. 65

9   Dr. Cindy Trimm, *Commanding your Morning* (Charisma House 2007) p. 2

10 Chip Ingram, *True Spirituality* (Howard Books 2009) p. 262, 270, 271

11 Ann Voscamp, *One Thousand Gifts* (Zondervan 2010) p. 72

12 http://brainyquote/quotes/melody_beattie134462

13 Ann Voscamp, *One Thousand Gifts* (Zondervan 2010) p. 91

14 http://theguardian.com/uk/2001/dec/20/humanities.research

15 Priscilla Shirer, *Fervent* (B&H Publishing Group 2015) p. 169

16 Priscilla Shirer, *Fervent* (B&H Publishing Group 2015) p. 170

17   Beth Moore, *So Long Insecurity* (Tyndale House, 2010) p. 280

18   Priscilla Shirer, *Fervent* (B&H Publishing Group, 2015) p. 151

19   http://radicalforgiveness.com/ unforgiveness-is-classified-in-medical-books-as-a-disease

20   http://whatyourfutureholds.wordpress. com /2009/01/29/the-harmfull-effects-of-unforgiveness

21   Ann Voscamp, *The Broken Way* (Zondervan, 2016) p. 188

22   Lisa Bevere, *Without Rival* (Revell / Baker Books, 2016) p. 20-21

23   Chip Ingram, *True Spirituality* (Howard, a division of Simon and Schuster 2009) p. 171

ALSO FROM DANIELLE:

GO DEEPER INTO GOD'S WORD

With a Bible study designed to help you recognize and
root-out the relationship spoilers in your own heart
while cultivating the ingredients for success!

About the Author

Danielle Macaulay is an author, blogger, speaker and television personality on the marriage television show, *A Better Us*. She is passionate about her marriage to her husband, recording artist Dan Macaulay, her two young boys, Keaton and Braden, and about helping women grow in their faith (she isn't afraid to admit she is also passionate about donuts, Hallmark movies and the spa). She provides regular nourishment for both your body and soul at her popular blog spot **frommilktomeat.com** and offers families spiritual nourishment and kid friendly recipes in her children's meal time devotional, *Table Talk: Family Dinner Devos*.

To book Danielle to speak at your event, contact:
info@daniellemacaulay.com

 / FromMilkToMeat

 / DanielleMacaulay80

OTHER WEBSITES TO CHECK OUT

- ◆ frommilktomeat.com
- ◆ danmac.org
- ◆ abetterus.tv